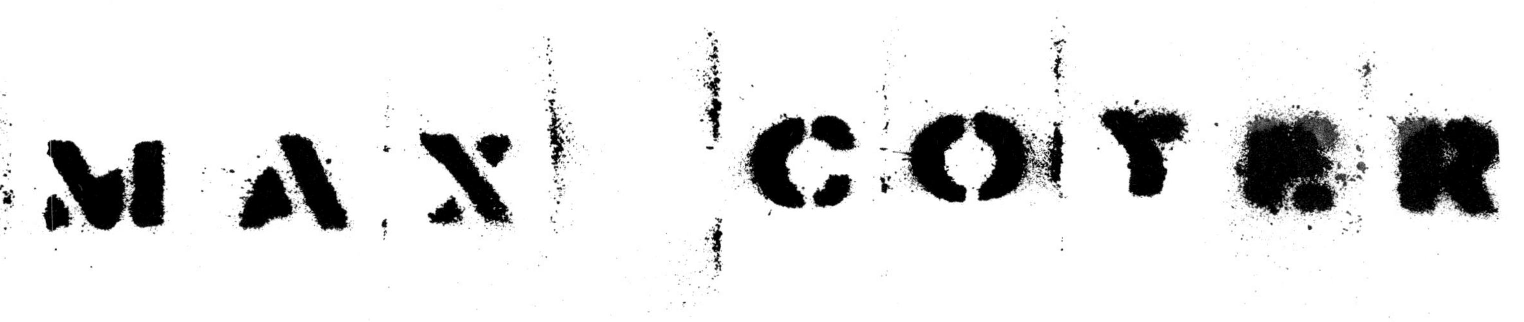


CURATOR: JUDY COLLISCHAN VAN WAGNER

**HILLWOOD ART GALLERY
LONG ISLAND UNIVERSITY
C.W. POST CAMPUS
BROOKVILLE, NEW YORK 11548**

Cover: *Annunciation,* 1987, oil on canvas, 60 x 72 " Courtesy Gruenebaum Gallery.

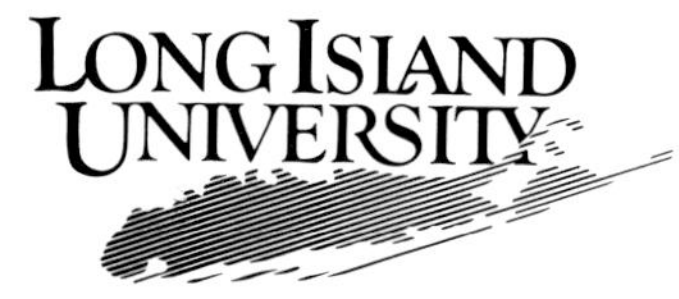

## LONG ISLAND UNIVERSITY

Dr. David J. Steinberg, President
Dr. David Newton, Executive Vice President
Mr. Ray Soldavin, Vice President of External Affairs
Mr. William Zeckendorf, Jr., Chairman, Board of Trustees
Dr. Doris Guidi, Provost, C.W. Post Campus

## HILLWOOD ART GALLERY

Dr. Judy Colischan Van Wagner, Director
Carol Becker Davis, Assistant Director
Judith Lintz, Secretary
Robert G. Van Wagner, Registrar
Academic Assistants:     Peter Klann
                         George Kourpas
                         Kimbrly Mund

**Library of Congress Cataloging-in-Publication Data**

Max Coyer.

    Exhibition held at Hillwood Art Gallery.
    Bibliography: p.
    Contents: Introduction — — Max Coyer: An Appreciation    /By Gary
Reynolds — — Max Coyer/By Reagan Upshaw — — Artist's Biography.
    1. Coyer, Max, 1954 —       Exhibitions. 2. Painting,     American — —
Exhibitions.     3.    Painting,    Modern — — 20th. Century — — United
States — — Exhibitions.     4.    Painters — — United States — — Biography.
I. Van Wagner, Judy K. Collischan.     II. Coyer, Max, 1954 —
III. Hillwood Art Gallery.
ND237.C813A4    1987    759.13(B)         87-32184
ISBN 0-933699-06-9

# TABLE OF CONTENTS

## ACKNOWLEDGMENTS

For their contributions to the publication of this book, we gratefully acknowledge the following individuals:

George Dalsheimer
Mr. & Mrs. Charles Fabrikant
Michael S. Frey
Fay Gold
Herman Greitzer
Tom Gruenebaum
Nanette L. Laitman
Carol & Ted S. Levy
Mr. & Mrs. Steven Molasky
Janet Nast
Robert Pearlstein
Mr. & Mrs. Mark K. Taylor

We also wish to credit photographer Ken Showell for his fine work and Christopher Makos for his portrait of Max Coyer.

Lastly, we would like to express our appreciation to the artist, Max Coyer, and to Harm Bouckaert, Director of the Gruenebaum Gallery, for their professional cooperation and assistance.

# INTRODUCTION

Five years ago, I chose Max Coyer's work for the "Painting from the Mind's Eye" exhibition held at Hillwood Art Gallery. This show examined visionary aspects present in the work of eight young painters. At that time, Max was engaged in a series of "cone" paintings involving an elementary form realized as part of a painterly field. Since then, he has explored a number of themes and subjects, many of them absorbed from the history of art.

With interest and pleasure, I have followed Coyer's steady progress as an artist that has not been matched by deserved critical attention. With this comprehensive exhibition, we aim to bring his talent, vision and commitment to a wider audience and to enhance his stature as an accomplished painter.

The title, "Icon and Iconography" was suggested by the Gallery's Assistant Director, Carol Becker Davis, who has also observed with admiration Coyer's escalating attainment and productivity. Essentially, we felt that the terms "icon" and "iconography" describe two prominent characteristics of Coyer's work. In a religious sense, an "icon" is the object of ritualistic devotion and meditation. Usually, the image is considered a sacred one and as such possessive of an impression of that supernatural power possessed by a godhead. From an historical viewpoint, the icon is a particular type of pictorial representation identifiable with specific cultures and their symbolic depictions. Characteristically, Coyer has adapted certain formal elements and materials of the icon into his own work. For instance, in his series of self-portraits, he has employed a bust semblance of himself silhouetted agianst a field of gold leaf. The artist's choice of media and format continue to evoke feelings of introspection and otherworldliness. His series of self portrayals constitute one portion of a personal lexicon of imagery and symbols developed throughout a large body of work. Coyer's individual iconography includes the cones and self-portraits as well as numerous motifs abstracted from the history of art, architecture and literature.

Among the prototypes selected by Coyer is that of the Wadsworth Atheneum court. His attachment to this subject is connected with childhood visits to the museum where he was attracted to architectural features of the structure as well as to work exhibited there by certain masters, such as Giorgio de Chirico. Subsequent to groups of work dealing with imagery from the Atheneum edifice and de Chirico picture, elements from these percepts recur in Coyer's oeuvre. Ingres' portraits, the self-portraits of Van Gogh and Picasso's Cubist renditions have likewise motivated consecutive clusters of work. Similarly, literary compositions like a play entitled *Madame de Sade* and Jean Cocteau's journal called *Opium* have inspired affectively powerful sequences of pictures.

The exhibition's origin and organization were resultantly dependent upon two respective factors: a continuing belief and confidence in the artist's importance and the desire to present his work in terms of its salient features. Intelligently, Coyer has observed his own encounters with art in formulating a distinctively singular body of work. Self-realization and external circumstance have been formalized in paintings that bear witness to an individual's experience and awareness. Thought and dream are interrelated and mutually informative within the context of Coyer's painted appearances. Coyer's work penetrates the edges of our consciousness. His paintings are discomforting and disturbing as they probe subliminal regions toward the pleasurable realm of insight.

JUDY COLLISCHAN VAN WAGNER

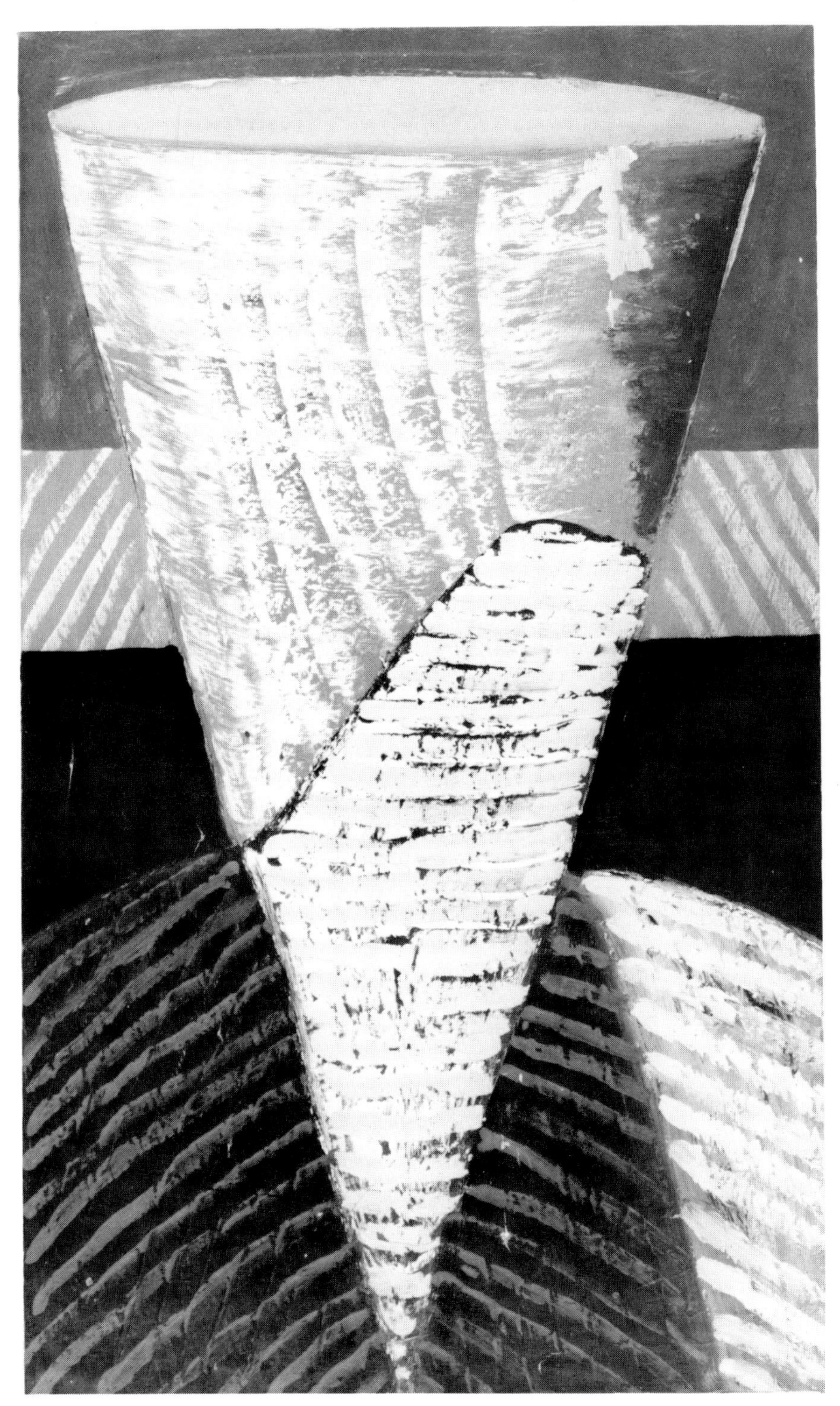

*Edo Cone,* 1982, oil on canvas, 48 x 28".

# MAX COYER: AN APPRECIATION

When I first saw Max Coyer's works a few years ago, I was immediately hooked. His use of art history was both fascinating and unexpected. The paintings were full of references that could be recognized but not in their usual contexts. Renaissance portraits locked horns with swirling geometric cones and African masks. One image poked out from under another, and then suddenly was hidden. This layering process created a palpable sense of time and movement; one could imagine the artist carefully laying in the silhouette of a Ingres portrait only to cover it over with a host of other references. All this might have been simply an elaborate game of art history — a kind of "Name That Tune" for erudite viewers — had the paintings not carried such emotional weight. The "portraits" had a brooding quality often quite at odds with the fascile, and frankly beautiful, paint surfaces. (The images from Coyer's "Madame de Sade" series, for example, can be both enticing and repellant.) For me, the emotional pitch of the artist's work hit its highest point in the "Jean Cocteau" paintings of 1985-86. Something of Cocteau's struggle both with his addiction and with his art came to the surface in Coyer's paintings. It was not just a matter of reusing Cocteau's images, but plumbing its very spirit. The artist's recent work has a more serene but nonetheless potent effect. The Buddha-like figure in "The Endless Voyage" paintings and the flowers of the recent still life series still leave one to look for the hidden messages and emotional undercurrents of the artist's vision. For me, it is still a most rewarding hunt.


GARY A. REYNOLDS  
Curator of Painting and Sculpture  
The Newark Museum

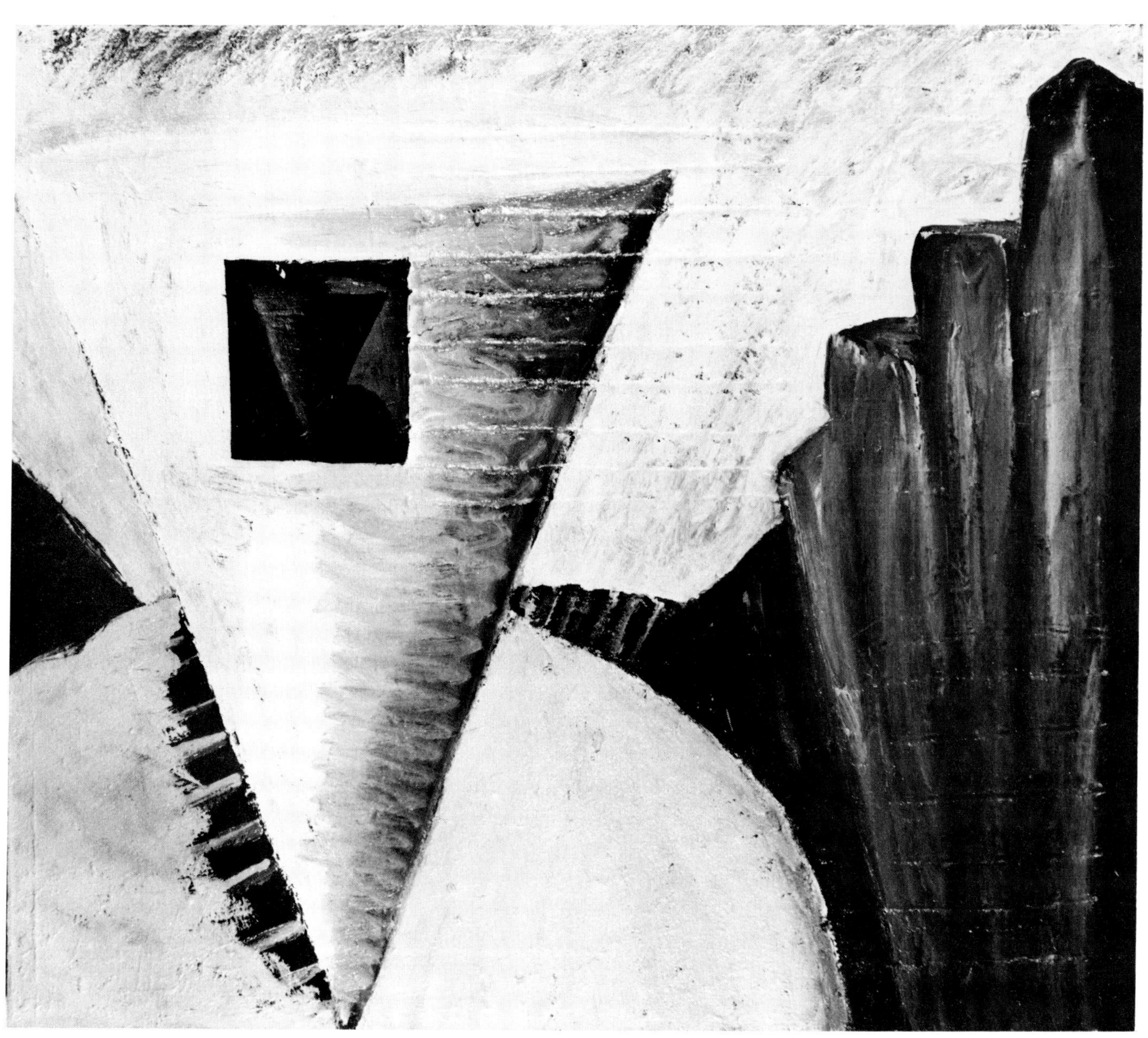

*Mantegna Cone,* 1982, oil on canvas, 48 x 54″.

# MAX COYER

Max Coyer is an artist who has squarely faced the most difficult problem confronting a painter today: given the history of painting, from the cave walls of Lascaux to the "White on White" of Malevich, how can an artist pick up a brush today and hope to discover anything new? If everything has already been done, what is the point of doing it yet again? Is the artist exploring uncharted territory, the task that modernism claimed for itself, or is he in our day reduced to making more or less pleasant items of decoration in the service of capitalism?

It is a daunting prospect. As Coyer has put it, "... as an artist working at the end of the twentieth century, subconsciously or consciously, there is the feeling of art history weighing down upon you. Every brushstroke you make on a canvas, someone else has made before you."[1] The works in this exhibition record Coyer's early realization that, "Art history is behind everything we do today," and his solution to the problem: "to actually use art history as subject matter."

Max Coyer was born in Hartford, Connecticut, in 1954. He attended the public schools, but more important to his growth as an artist was the visual education he acquired for himself at the Wadsworth Atheneum. His mother would drop the boy off at the museum while she did her shopping, and by the time he was 10, he had become intimately acquainted with works by masters ranging from Cranach to De Chirico. Coyer drew and painted avidly while in grade school, but when it came time for college, he opted to major in English at Trinity College in Hartford. At Trinity, he concentrated on twentieth century poetry. After two years, the call of New York became overwhelming, and the young man was off. In the city, he found a welcome on the half-bohemian, half-fashionable fringes of the art world. More important, he decided to return to painting.

In 1978, at the age of 24, Coyer began a series which he in retrospect feels are his first important works of art: pencil drawings of objects of daily life — tooth brushes, tape dispensers, loose cigarettes, and others. The objects, though mundane, often had an air of mystery or psychological tension in their presentation. In one, for example, a telephone is seen from behind on a pedestal or night table with an address book, seen from on end, beside it. The cradle of the phone is empty; the cord to the receiver stretches off to the right and out of the drawing. A call is obviously being made, but by whom and for what purpose? In other drawings, toothbrushes, with the assistance of diagrammatic lines, meet, are banished, and engage in intrigues of an almost erotic nature. The drawings themselves are rendered in a very precise, deadpan style, but the objects they portray are capable of surprisingly touching voices.

Coyer moved from these drawings into a series of paintings. Although the images were totally abstract, elements in them were derived from artworks of the past. One painting, for example, had a composition loosely based on a crucifixion by Lucas Cranach the Elder. Coyer had realized by this time that "... the only way an artist can work today is to make synthetic art or art derived from the work of someone else."[2] Synthetic art became a byword with Coyer. It was derived from Hegel's formula: thesis-antithesis-synthesis. In Coyer's view, the thesis of modernism had been grounded in nineteenth century academic art, typified by the artists of the French Academy. The School of Paris — Picasso, Matisse, and their followers — had been the antithesis to the Academy, a rebellion that continued through the Abstract Expressionist movement. But how far can one rebel? The academics had been thoroughly defeated by modernism, and the progression from figurative art to abstraction had proceeded with the inevitability of *The Origin of Species.* As Minimal Art in the 1960s carried modernism to its logical conclusion, painting was declared to have run its course and become obsolete. But painting refused to die, and to Coyer the only way to continue to paint that was not thoroughly retardataire was by means of an art that declared the split between academic art and modernism to be at an end and took both areas as fields equally available for gleaning.

It was not, however, merely "high art" that was open to appropriation. Coyer had learned well the lessons that Warhol and the other Pop artists had to teach. Images from popular culture, and especially from television, had an undeniable impact upon society's visual sense and should therefore be as available to the artist as a madonna by Raphael. Synthetic art did not fight against the past, but rather embraced it. Neither did synthetic art have modernism's obsession with the ever-new; the question of how to be continually modern was declared moot.

But Coyer was not entirely free of modernism's seriousness of purpose. The abstract paintings began to seem to him to be pleasant exercises in composition, but little more. "Decorative," that dirty word of modernism, came to be the judgment he applied to them. Coyer had no interest in making merely decorative art. The works would have to be destroyed.

The cycle of paintings that destroyed the abstract works — literally, as we shall see — came about as the result of a dream. For all of Coyer's erudition and clear-headedness in terms of aesthetic theory, his bent is essentially romantic, and he has given great credence to dreams at crucial points in his career. In the dream that started the new series, Coyer was flying in a space ship in the shape of a cone. The ship moved in a peculiar fashion — first the point of the cone would stretch ahead of the rest of the ship, then the rest of the ship would snap forward to keep up with the nose. Coyer found the image so striking that he began a series of paintings, each depicting a single cone, point down. To the sides of each cone was the arc of a circle. The result could be read as a cone spinning on the top of a round table. In an anthropomorphic sense, however, the cone could be read as an abstract head with the circle's arc as two shoulders, and the artist, like almost everyone else, found it natural to refer to these paintings as "Cone Heads."

The paintings were done over the abstract paintings that had gone before. This was in part an economy measure, as Coyer at the time lacked the money for new canvases, but he also found that the new paintings gained from the underlying works. The underlying layers of color were often visible through the new layers; indeed, when Coyer was painting and the paint was still wet, he had no way of knowing what the final coloration would be. In "Cranach the Elder," for example, the artist was laying fresh gray paint over turquoise and did not know how much of the gray would be absorbed by the turquoise. Like a potter glazing a pot and putting it into the kiln, Coyer would see the final result only when the work was dried and set. In the same way, the underlying texture of the impasto and built-up areas had to be struggled with in making the new paintings. Usually Coyer made no concessions to them in laying on the new image. Traces of the old compositions remain, making the paintings like palimpsests and adding complexity and richness to each image.

It is remarkable how much variation Coyer was able to achieve in a relatively simple format. Some of the cones are rendered with only the barest suggestion of three-dimensionality; others receive a chiaroscuro that practically makes them leap off the canvas. Likewise, the variations in the "shoulders" impart a wide range of psychological impact, depending upon whether their edges extend to the edge of the canvas. Some Coneheads are diffident; others shoulder their way into an aggressive confrontation.

The titles of the paintings are enigmatic, relating primarily to private correspondences the artist made between them and other works of art. "Cranach the Elder," for example, has a ridge of paint running diagonally from the upper right. This is a remnant of the painting which underlies it, one of whose compositional elements was inspired by the odd angle of the Tau cross in the crucifixion by that German artist. "Toledo Cone," on the other hand, was so named because the coloration reminded Coyer of the coloration in El Greco's "Storm Over Toledo."

Coyer stopped the Conehead series after about thirty works. He found them to be getting "too easy and too abstract."[3] There followed a period of about six months where he did not paint, as he thought through various means to escape the impasse. As an alternative, he began a series of photographs of nude male torsos. They were an exploration of the apprehension of the male figure. The nude female figure has been the very stuff of Western art, whether surrounded by mythological trappings or with a more frankly erotic intent. The situation of male nudity, on the other hand, has been quite different, whether because of homophobia or other reasons. The reception of the photographs at their 1983 exhibition convinced Coyer that the subject is still far from neutral. Aside from the sociological lessons they had to teach, the photographs were important in habituating Coyer to the human figure as art, a subject that had not occurred in his mature work before. Thus they opened the way for his Wadsworth Atheneum series.

The Wadsworth Atheneum paintings were the result of a merging of art history and Coyer's biography. Ready for new paintings and wanting them not to be totally abstract, he decided to bring his influences to the surface.

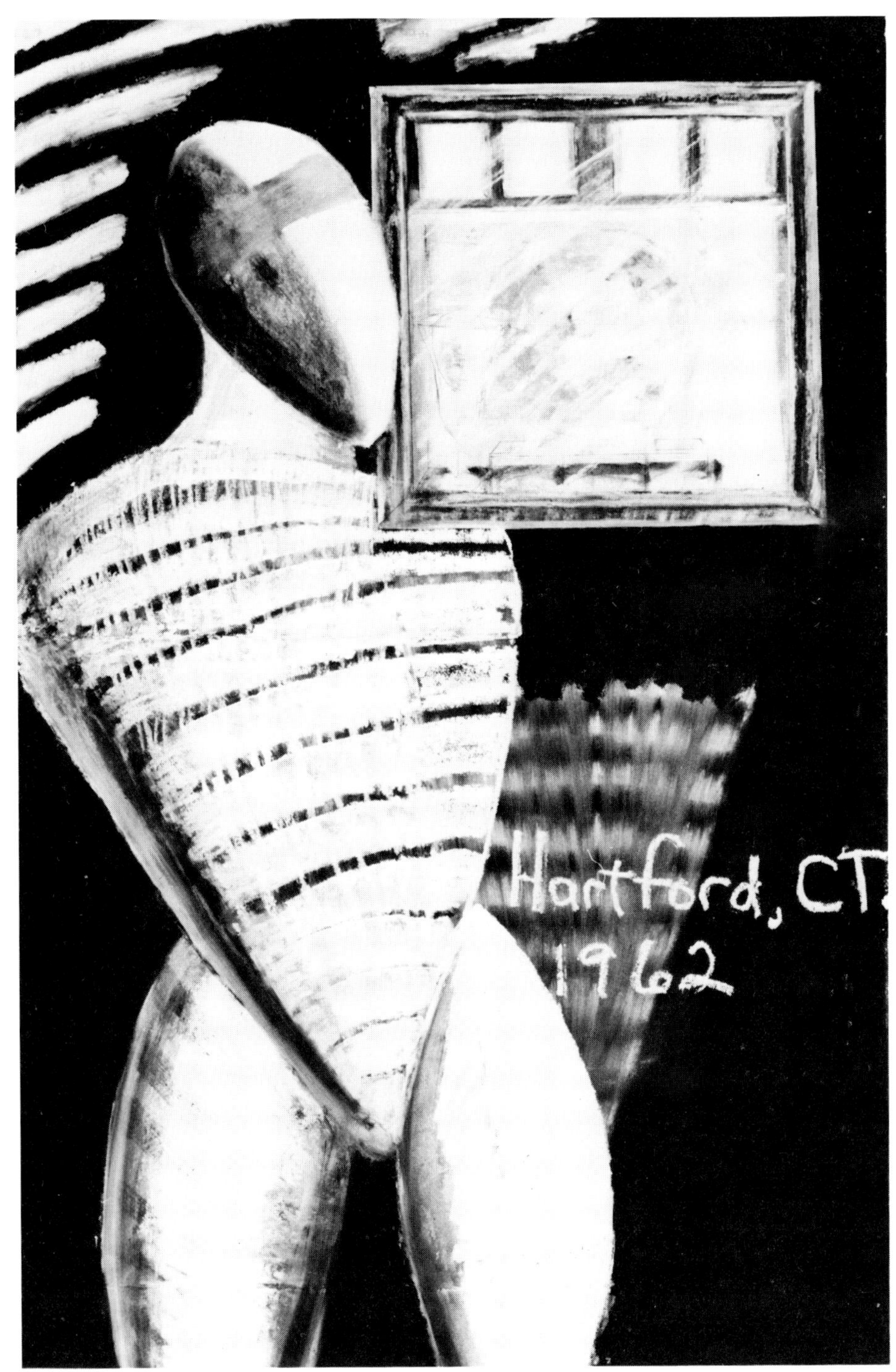



*Perceiving Cornell*, 1983, oilstick and pastel on paper, 46 1/2 x 30".

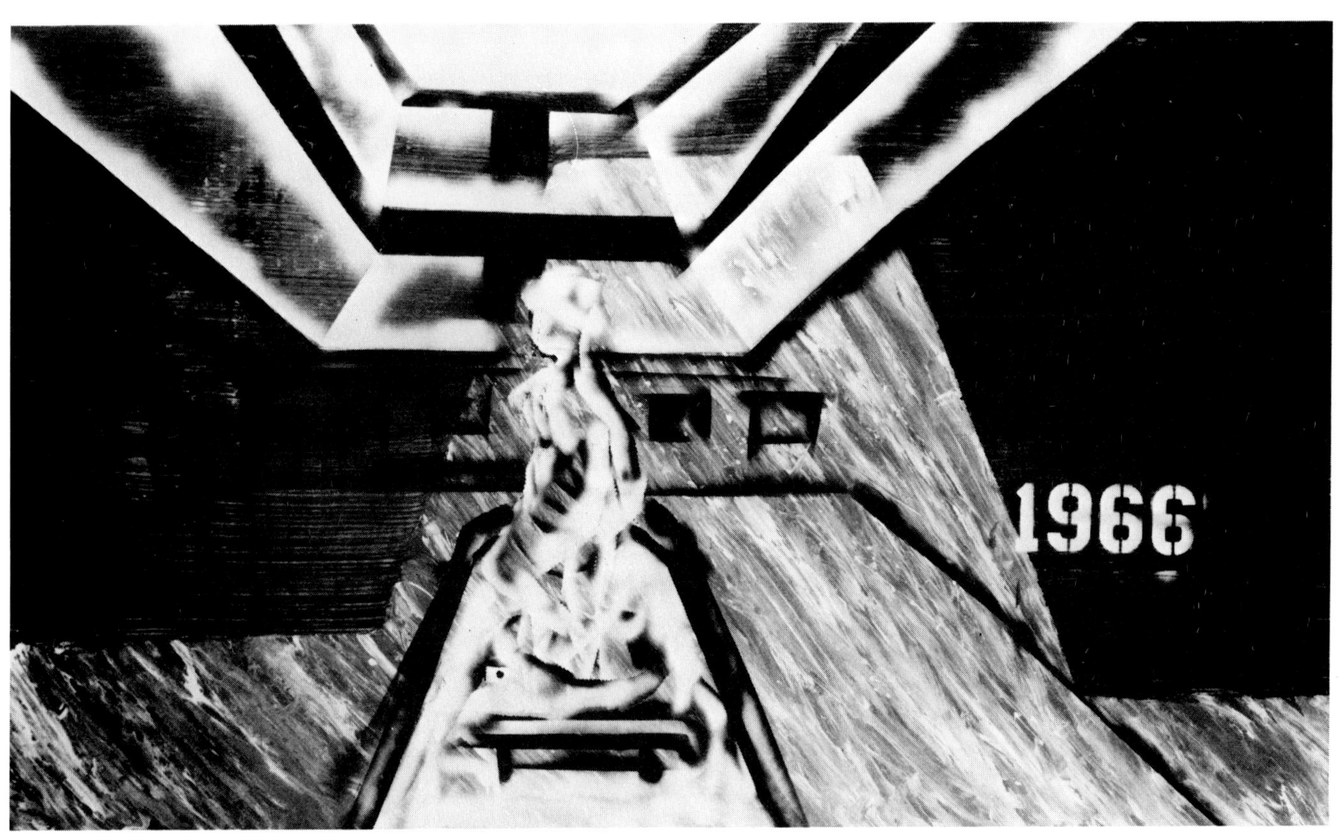

*Avery Court - 1966*, 1983, oil on canvas with spray enamel, 48 x 82". Collection Mr. & Mrs. Ted Levy.

If there were certain influences hidden underneath the surface of the cone paintings, why shouldn't I make that my subject matter? The more I thought about it, the more valid a concern it seemed to be, and I felt liberated with this realization. If you love De Chirico and you have an instinct to paint like he did, then you're totally liberated when you can make a facsimile. I thought back on my childhood as to which works of art had been most powerful to me then. I chose from the collection of the Wadsworth Atheneum, because that's what I had seen as a youth.[4]

So Coyer began to take quotes almost verbatim from his favorite works. De Chirico's "The Endless Voyage" was an immediate appropriation. So were works such as Lucas Cranach the Elder's "Feast of Herod" and the boxes of Joseph Cornell. The series forced Coyer to recall in detail his visits to the museum. Certain artists, such as De Chirico, had attracted him at first sight; others, such as Cornell, had at first proved baffling and unattractive. The dates that Coyer stencilled onto his new canvases were the dates that, thinking back, Coyer felt that he had achieved a real appreciation of the artist.

In this series, Coyer employed his modus operandi of painting, destroying, and repainting. An image would be laid on, then effaced by overpainting or scraping away part of the image, then a new image would be painted beside or slightly over the remnant, with both new and old images informing and enriching each other. The paintings were at once impersonal and autobiographical. On the one hand, the constituent images were drawn from the vast store of Western art history, available to anyone; on the other, they were a record of the artist's education. Even this record, however, was treated with detachment: the dates, enigmatic enough in themselves, were not added by the artist's hand, but rather stencilled on. (In like fashion, Coyer later began to stencil his name on the face of the canvas. He had always signed them on the reverse, but came to feel that the artist's identity is as much a part of the visual information as anything else in the painting.)

The Wadsworth Atheneum series also incorporates a medium that Coyer has since abandoned: spray paint. At the time — 1983 — that the works were being done, graffiti artists were the rage of the trendy art scene. Galleries such as the now-defunct F.U.N. Gallery were presenting the works of poor kids from the Bronx, some of them not out of their teens, and more than one writer proclaimed them the true heirs of Pollock. Coyer was intrigued with the "new" medium of spray paint. Unlike the graffiti artists, however, he did not spray on the paint in undisciplined fashion; instead, using a piece of cardboard as a border, he literally drew with the paint. The images thus executed are so controlled that they sometimes have the appearance of having been stencilled on, but this was not the case. The outlines produced, where one side of the line is relatively straight and sharp and the other wavers in and out, flicker with a mysterious light. Coyer used the technique in this and some of the later series, but later came to feel that he had exploited to the limit the possibilities of spray paint in this fashion.

That and the health hazards associated with the medium caused him to give it up.

1984 saw three related groups of paintings. The first group might be called variations of the portrait of Dora Maar by Picasso. The second group was the Madame de Sade series, based upon a group of female portraits by Ingres. The third group, "Technicians of Ecstacy," were based on male portraits by various artists.

The Dora Maar paintings, with one exception, are based upon a Picasso portrait with which Coyer was taken in his early teens; he had a poster of the work in his room. (The exception in the series is based upon a different portrait of Maar.) They are thus related to the Wadsworth Atheneum series in that they are in part a reflection upon works that influenced Coyer in his youth. At the same time, taken with the Madame de Sade series, tey were almost didactic, a meditation upon the image of woman that permeates French art in a fashion that it does in the art of almost no other country.[5]

The paintings again use the technique of creation, destruction, and reconstitution. Picasso's Dora, enlarged to over twice her original size, is laid in, scraped away, and repainted. The titles are often fanciful — "Alien Culture," for example — but sometimes they take on topical meanings. One Dora seemed when finished to be wearing a blindfold. The painting was done shortly after the murder of four American nuns in El Salvador, and Coyer's painting became "The Nun."

The "Madame de Sade" title is at first misleading. The women who inhabit these paintings were the subjects of famous portraits by Ingres — the Countess d'Haussonville, the Princess de Broglie, and others. There is no portrait by Ingres of Madame de Sade; indeed, the wife of the notorious marquis had died before Ingres began painting. She had been loyal to her husband while he was in prison, but had left him upon his release. Madame de Sade functions as a sort of White Goddess for Coyer. Her name "gave an aura of depth to a female figure," according to the artist. Certainly the name of de Sade arouses associations, ominous or otherwise, in every mind. Is she a ministrant of pain, pleasure, or both? It is tempting to establish links to the artist: if she is his nurturer and muse, is he de Sade, the cruel one? Again and again, in the works to come, Coyer will draw parallels between himself and creative personalities who are, for one reason or another, beyond the pale of bourgeois society.

The compositional format of the works is fairly uniform — a three-quarter length female, faceless, but with enough fidelity to the famous poses of Ingres's models to be instantly recognizable. Coyer was intrigued with the fact that although Ingres's sitters appear to have been relatively insipid he was able to create powerful portraits of them. In Coyer's paintings, the lack of facial features mimics the models' vapidity, yet Madame commands her space, serenely indifferent to accessories such as pillars which may crowd in, the letters which sometimes share the space, and the lines that zip across her. The zips in this series grow out of the underlying ridges of paint of the Conehead series. Coyer uses the stripes to deny illusionism and insist on the flatness of the picture plane. At the same time, he often uses stripes to form a sort of frame within the frame. He has always delighted in setting up and then undermining illusion. Some of the stripes are laid over what has already been painted, gaining by their very thickness the sense of being around and on top of the enclosed painting; others, however, are laid in at earlier stages of the composition and are left in place, instead of being painted over, while the painting grows around them. This accounts for the constant "push-pull" of paint often found on his surfaces. He paints thinly, with his oil much diluted with turpentine, causing many drips and runs. These are left in or painted out according to how the artist feels they help the painting.

The third of the 1984 series relates to the Madame de Sade works, except that figures are drawn from portraits by other artists, such as Bronzino or Rembrandt. The figures are male, and in place of a face Coyer has substituted a mask derived from African art. the resultant figures — a Bronzino torso abstracted and topped with a Dogon mask, for example — gain an eerie, otherworldly quality from the juxtaposition, an effect Coyer augments by giving the works such titles as "Forest Spirit" or "Figure of the Night." The overall title for the group, "Technicians of Ecstacy," relates to and in fact is another term for shamans. They are the persons with magical powers who intermediate between us and the supernatural. Male shamans were left behind fairly early in Western Culture, while the female ones stayed in the form of witches. Coyer brings the male shaman back, another example of his continuing attempt to take something of Western painting's obsession with the female figure and transfer it to the male. At the same time, the works, with their borrowing from primary art and grafting it onto new Western stock, belong solidly to the modernist tradition dating back at least to Picasso's "Les Demoiselles d'Avignon."

For a Chicago exhibition, Coyer did a series of works, some based upon De Chirico and some on Caravaggio. His return to De Chirico was in part a re-opening of the examination of his childhood (indeed, one wonders whether an overall title for Coyer's oeuvre might be, to adapt a title from Wordsworth, "Intimations of Aesthetics from Recollections of Early Childhood"). It was in part a continuation of an earlier aesthetic concern: the cone. De Chirico's triangular figures reminded Coyer in some way of the Coneheads. Coyer's use of them was also a part of what might be called his continuing exploration of genres. In the 19th century academic scheme of things, there were several genres of paintings, such as allegorical or religious painting, historical paintings, landscapes, portraits, and still lifes. Allegorical or religious painting was ranked the highest, because it supposedly required the greatest amount of invention on the part of the artist. Still life painting ranked lowest, as the artist was merely imitating what was already there and no invention was required. In his portraits, Coyer had already explored one genre; in the new De Chirico-based works, he explored the tradition of the figure in a landscape. (The works are not based solely upon De Chirico, by the way; references to artists as diverse as Georges de la Tour and Max Ernst also creep in.) In addition to being landscapes with figures, the paintings draw on what has today become another genre: surrealism. With the passing of the Surrealist (with a capital S) movement and the collapse of modernism's forced march towards historical necessity, the surrealist style has merely become one

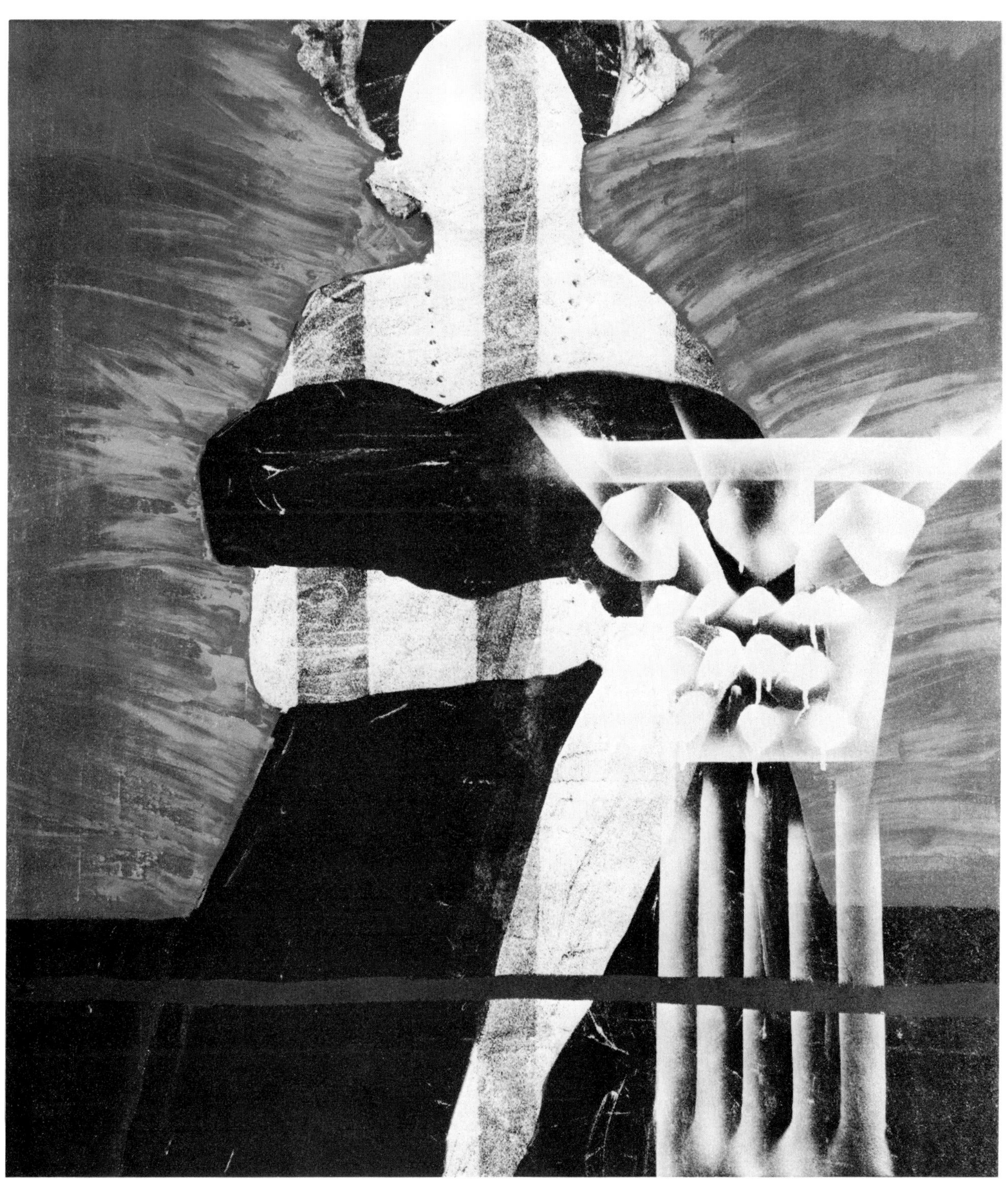

*Madame de Sade #1*, 1984, oil and spray enamel on canvas, 42 x 36". Private Collection.

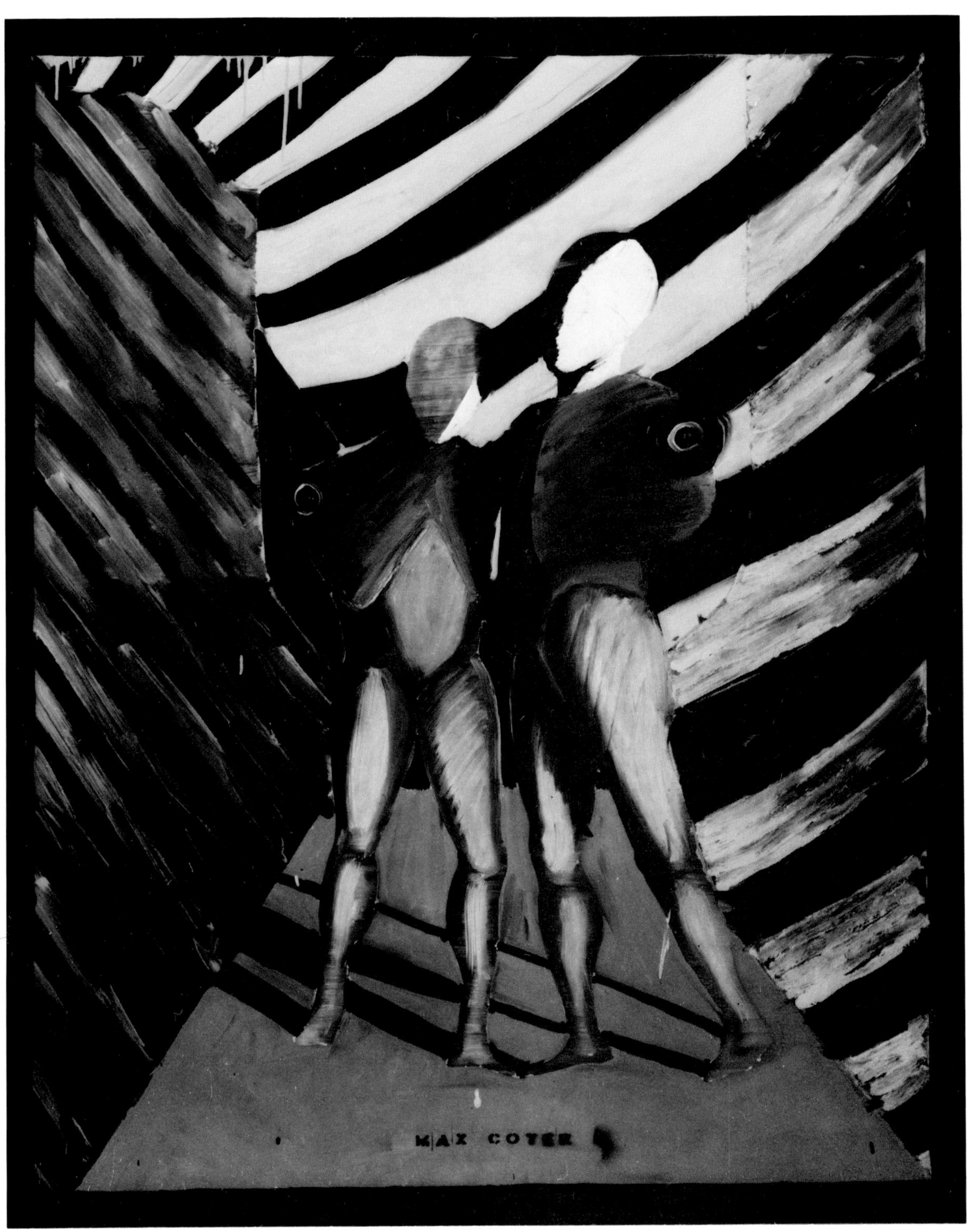



*Large Double de Chirico,* 1984, oil on canvas, 60 x 48″.

more method for the artist to use when he wishes to achieve a certain effect. Coyer's De Chiricos were stripped of their original context and made into elements in a new aesthetic scheme. Yet they also managed at times to convey some of their original unease as they played their new roles.

In Caravaggio, one senses that Coyer must have felt a kindred spirit. Although living almost two centuries before the romantic era, Caravaggio is in many ways the prototype of the artist as romantic hero. Proud, rebellious, fiercely individualistic, and often on the outs with his patrons, Caravaggio burst onto the artistic world of Rome, introduced a new style of art that would influence artists for years to come, and then died young. Homoeroticism pervades many of his best-known paintings, such as "Bacchus" and "Amor Vincit Omnia." "Bacchus," with its slightly effeminate youth, dolled up like a geisha and proferring a glass of wine is the gay pin-up par excellence. Coyer removes the figure from its context and lets a stripped-down version preside over the revels.

From the kindred spirit of Caravaggio, Coyer moved on to the work of another kindred spirit, Jean Cocteau. The Wadsworth Atheneum had an exhibition of the French artist's drawings when Coyer was young, and the memory of the show doubtless infused his choice of subject. At the same time, there were fascinations of character: Cocteau was witty, ironic, adept with both word and brush; unlike Caravaggio, he was a charming rebel, at home both in fashionable society and the demi-monde. In 1929 Cocteau had entered a clinic to rid himself of an addiction to opium and as a part of his treatment had done a series of self portraits.

Cocteau's drawings were about the agonies of withdrawal from drugs. Coyer felt that the works could serve as metaphors for today's artistic withdrawal from the tenets of modernism after "modernism became a habit."[6] The figures depicted somewhat resemble Leger's tubular figures, but the tubes from which Cocteau had constructed them were opium pipes. The strange figures were now to find themselves rendered in oil and placed in an unfamiliar setting, as distinct from Cocteau's unadorned backgrounds. As backgrounds for the figures, Coyer preferred a boxed-in, claustrophobic space. Like Baudelaire, who wrote of obsession, disgust, and despair in impeccable alexandrines, Coyer takes the cold-turkey shakes of Cocteau and puts them into an academic, almost classical setting. In "The Death of Vitellius," for example, the toga-clad figure, appropriate for a roman emperor, was actually taken from Cocteau. In the middle of the figure can be seen the outline of a bound hand, taken from the painting of the same title by Jules-Eugene Lenepveu, a nineteenth century French artist. The architecture is taken from Tintoretto's "Finding of Saint Mark." Barely visible is the hind leg of a horse from an equestrian portrait by Velasquez. Some description of the execution of this painting is in order, as it was typical of Coyer's working method. He began with the large, toga-clad figure from Cocteau. he next painted in the horizontal figure from Lenepveu, intending to have a cruciform composition, but he found that the resulting composition did not work and subsequently painted out most of the figure of Vitellius, leaving only the hands. The architecture was then added to give a more complex spatial sense to the work.

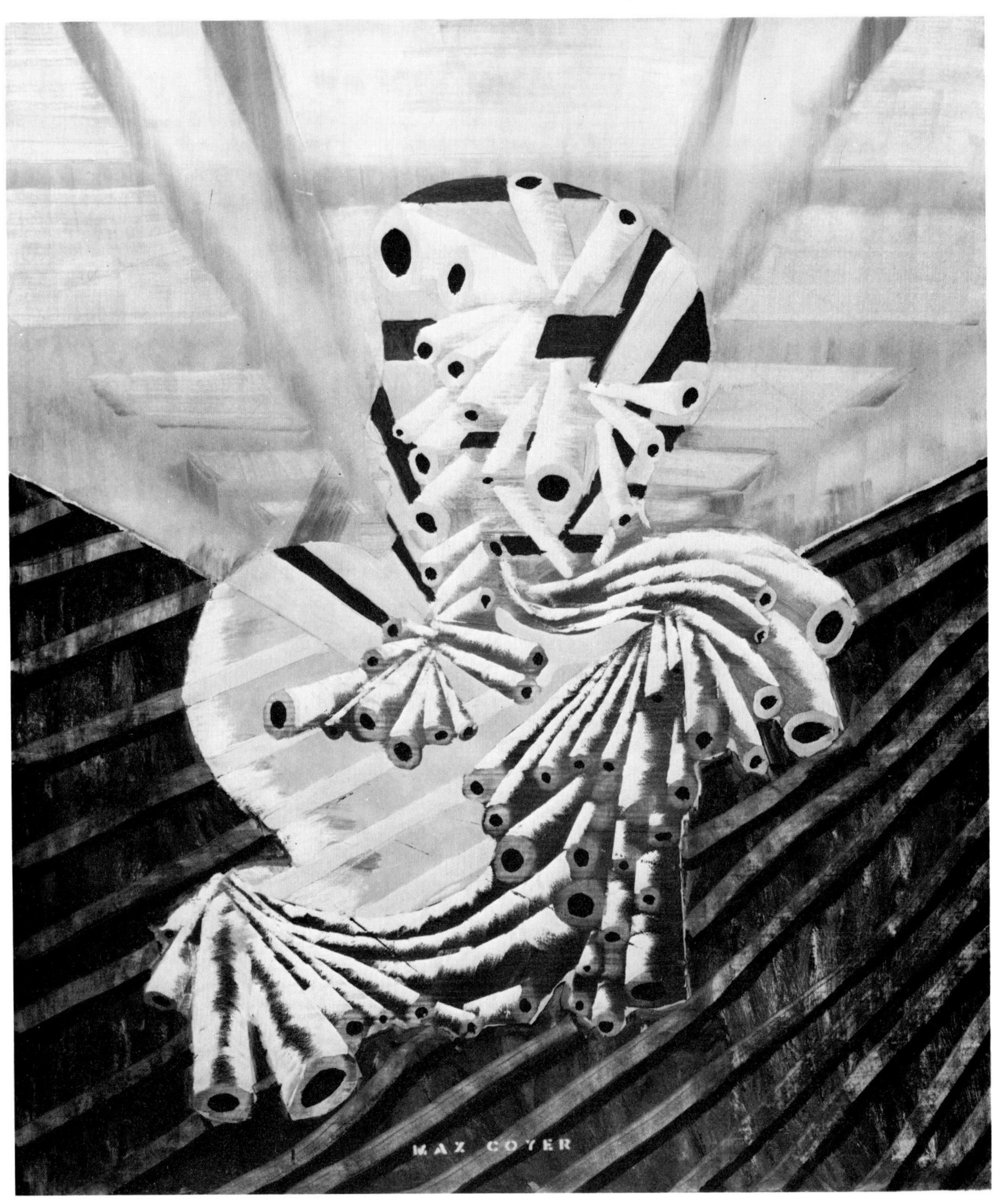

*Star Thrower*, 1985, oil on canvas, 60 x 48".

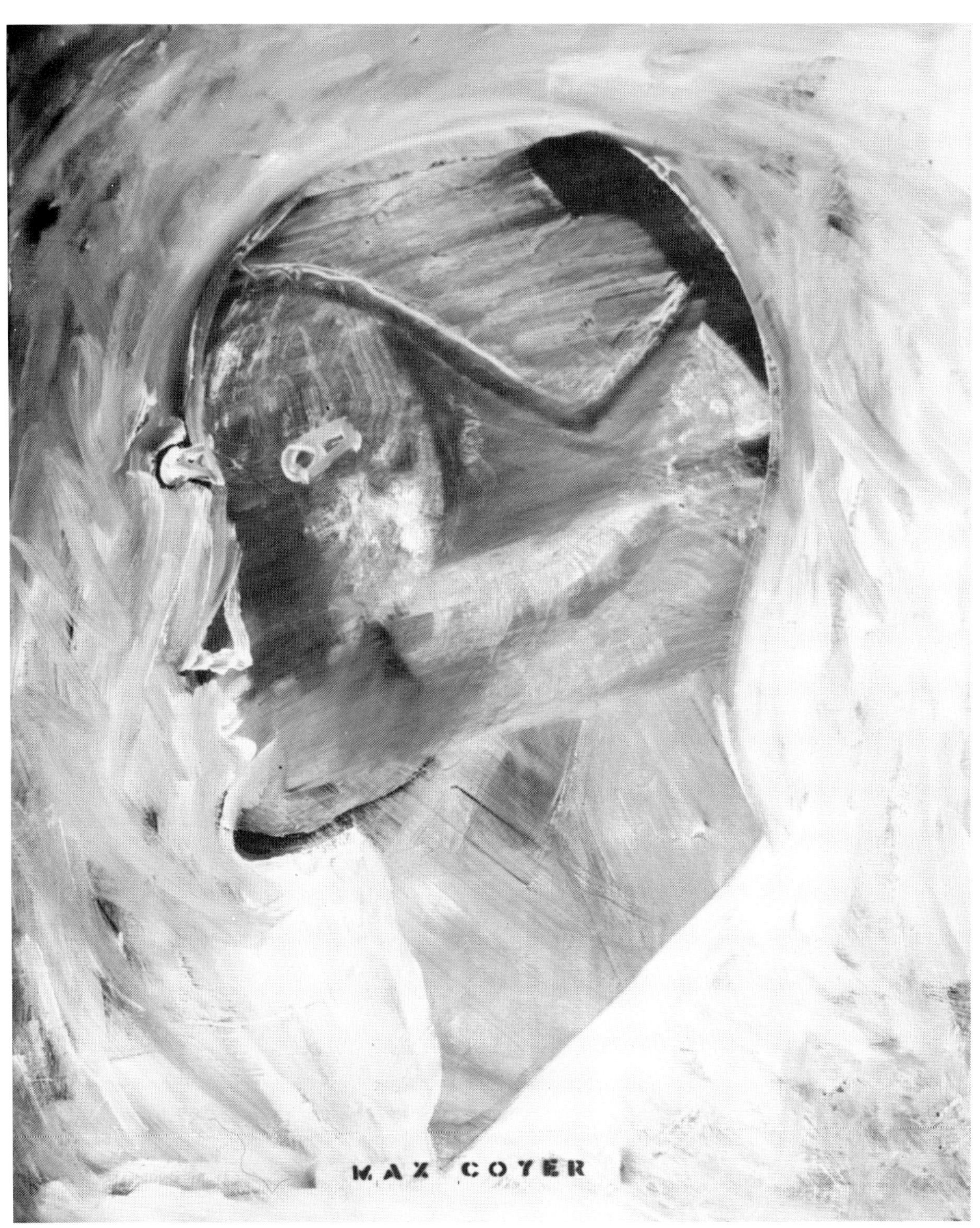


*Opium Bird,* 1985, oil on canvas, 44 x 34". Collection Mr. Robert Pearlstein.

Finally Coyer tried to work the horse into the composition, but again was unsatisfied with the result and expunged most of the figure. Color was then added or altered to unify the resultant composition. Coyer may be seen, therefore, as almost a collagiste. He has spoken of his dissatisfaction with purely abstract art, at least when not informed with the underlying philosophy of a Mondrian. Instead, he works with figurative elements in an abstract fashion.

Certainly the general viewer will not recognize all of the allusions in these works; even the art historian would be hard-pressed to identify all of the quotations. But in "The Death of Vitellius" and the other works of the series, the viewer must certainly sense that a great deal of visual information is being simultaneously revealed and suppressed, that other works of art are being incorporated into the work, and that the painting is as much about the history of art as the present depiction of a strong image.

One of Cocteau's drawings presented a male, lying on his back on a bed or examining table, head hanging over the edge toward the viewer, eyes bulging with exertion or pain. Coyer used this figure in a few paintings of the series that introduced another titan from our aesthetic history: Frank Lloyd Wright. Coyer juxtaposes Cocteau's figure with Wright's architecture: in "Johnson's Wax," the male is impaled upon the famous columns of Wright's Racine building; in "Falling Water," he is crushed between the slabs of Wright's most famous residence.

More will be said about Wright in connection with a later series of paintings, but one might speculate here about his juxtapoistion with Cocteau. Cocteau has been viewed with suspicion in some circles; he has been seen as a flighty dilettante, constantly flitting between art, writing, and film, and never sufficiently serious. Wright, on the other hand, was quite successful in getting the art world to take him as seriously as he took himself. A megalomaniac with a fight for self-promotion, he was an authentic genius and one of the founders of modernism in architecture. He had none of Cocteau's or Coyer's wit (or self-doubt?), and I suspect that Coyer admires his self-confidence and his ability, while at the same time realizing that Wright was one of the leaders of the modernism which has become a habit. Is it coincidence that his works oppress Cocteau's self-portrait? Coyer seems to regard Wright with a sort of appalled fascination, but he does not take sides in this thesis-antithesis confrontation; rather, Coyer tries to create a synthesis. Cocteau's opium-pipe figures were so complicated in themselves that they were difficult to use in conjunction with a second figure, but Coyer found Wright's architecture simple yet strong enough to hold its own with the large figures.

Along with the Cocteau-inspired paintings, Coyer exhibited a series of ten "icons." The artist has said that the works were inspired by a dream; he heard a voice telling him to make ten of them, that nine of them were to be human, the tenth a horse, and that they were to be hung high. Some of the icons are obvious — Cocteau, both as a young and as an old man — others were more mysterious, such as "Icon of Waiting." Like the icons from the Middle Ages, their backgrounds are leafed with gold, its elegance making a sharp contrast with the ramshackle nature of their plywood supports. Unlike the icons, their function is enigmatic: the figures are being presented in somewhat the same format as religious works, but there is no clue as to how we are to approach these figures. Coyer thus sets up a double distortion: prototypical icons are religious objects, serving almost as stand-ins for God or the saint depicted, and with a traditional format and medium. Coyer, though invoking the object of adoration, ignores or subverts it, and his paintings are done almost in indifference to the jury-rigged structure of the wooden support. In this aspect, they may be considered along with the following series, a group of self portraits done in 1986. In their three-dimensionality, they almost qualify as wall sculpture. Coyer constructed and gessoed the wood supports first, without a concern for the images that would be painted over them. (All of this, of course, has obvious parallels in his earlier works, most notably the Conehead series, where the works were done without a concern for the designs and ridges of the previous works that were painted over.)

If the paintings are at odds with their supports, so are they at odds with their genre, for these self portraits are not of Coyer, but are rather based on the famous "Self-Portrait Dedicated to Paul Gauguin," painted by Vincent Van Gogh in 1888. Coyer was struck by the resemblance between Van Gogh's and his own features: "You see a picture of yourself, and it isn't you." In these works we have the

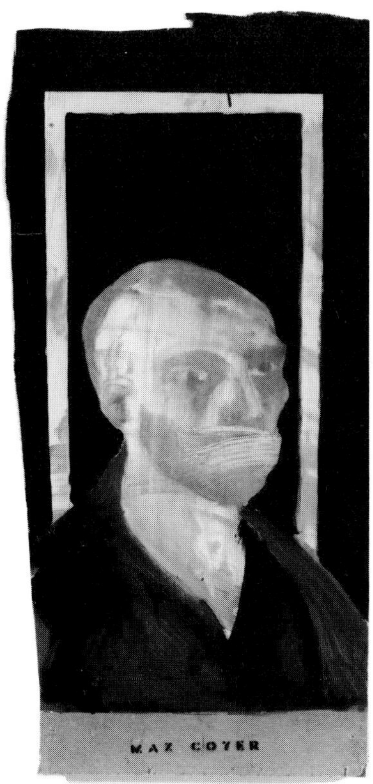

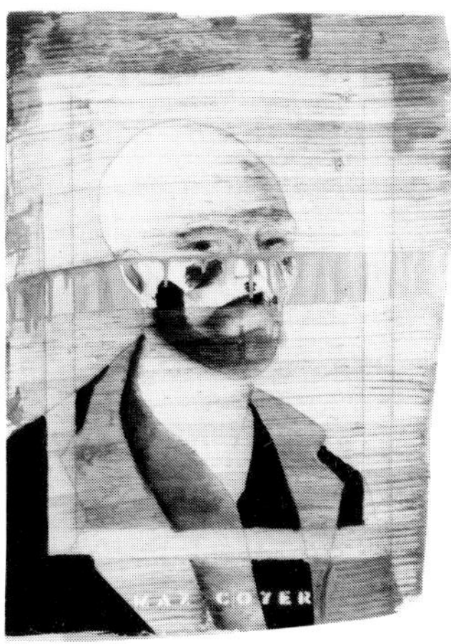

Left: *Self-Portrait #2,* 1986, oil on wood with gold leaf, 48 x 26".

Right: *Self-Portrait #6,* 1986, oil on wood, 21 x 27".

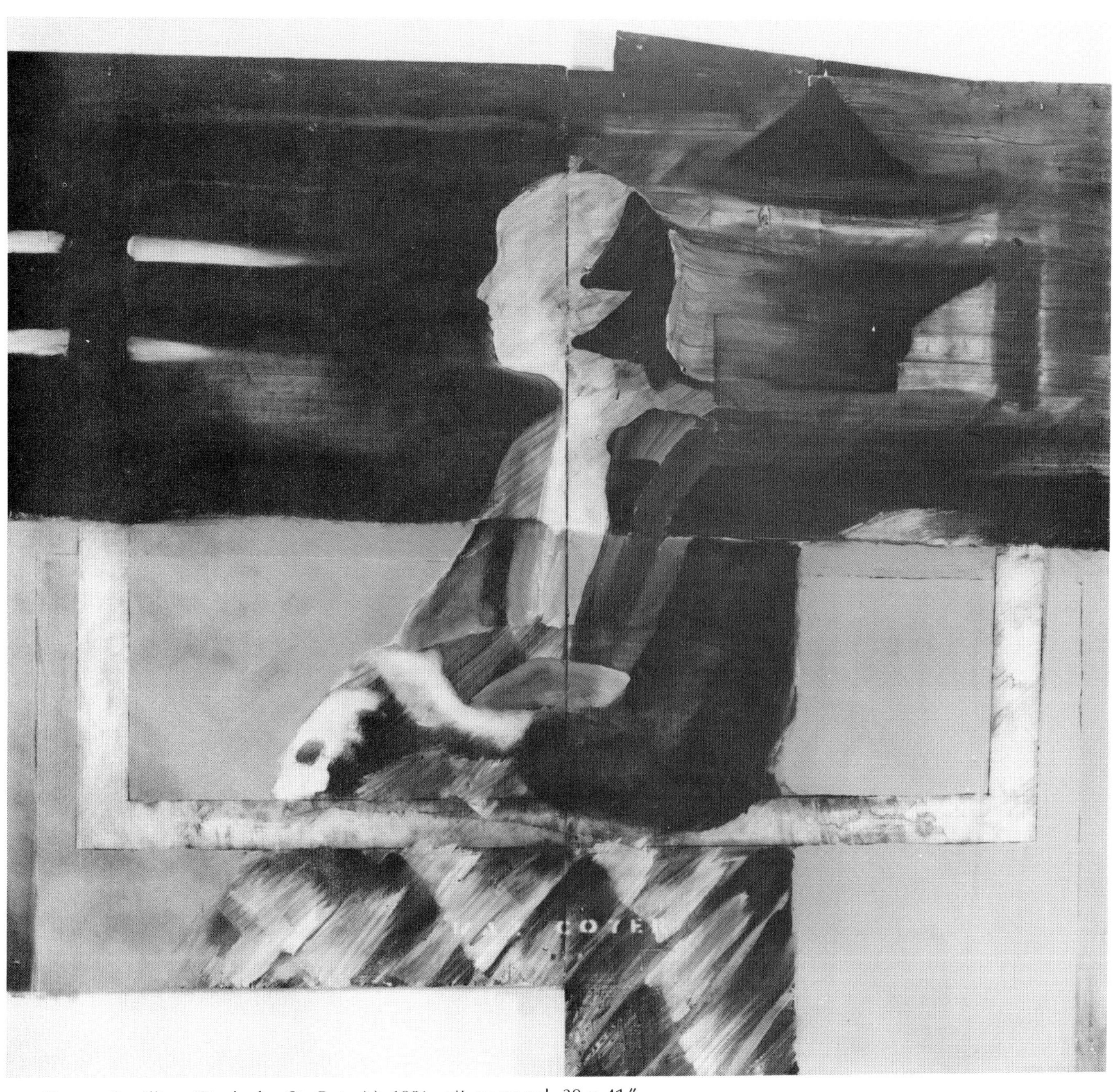

*Dream Pavillion* (Study for St. Peter's), 1986, oil on panel, 39 x 41".

artist as tortured Romantic hero and the artist as image appropriator. The face of the earlier artist becomes both witness of experience and substitute for experience. These are self portraits once removed.

In 1986 Coyer was invited to do an installation at St. Peter's church, an Episcopal church located in the Citicorp complex in Manhattan. In keeping with the environment, he chose to do a work with a religious theme. The work was entitled "The Endless Voyage: Death and Transfiguration." The eleven-foot painting fits into the tradition of an altarpiece with two wings. In the central panel, two enigmatic figures confront each other. Both figures were derived from "The Penitent Magdalene" by Georges de la Tour, here transmuted into an androgynous, almost Buddha-like figure that confronts itself reversed. Coyer had been struck, in reading literature on death, by the experience, reported by many persons who had been clinically dead but revived, that the soul after death turns and sees the body it has just left. The two figures may be taken as soul and body, but the artist has left unclear the question of which figure is which. The left-hand figure appears more solid; it rests "on top" of the canvas, while the figure on the right is informed by the colors around it; it is created by use of negative space. One might thus take the left-hand figure to be the body, but it is poised before a pagoda. Coyer uses the pagoda as a metaphor for death in human experience, for it is familiar and mysterious at the same time. This style of architecture is familiar to the average Western viewer, but, on the other hand, he has no idea of what its interior is — how many rooms, how they are laid out, and so on. The right-hand figure could therefore be the body emptied of life and confronted by its new, now-more-real soul from the vantage of death. The artist does not insist on either interpretation. Coyer, as usual, makes a bow to his past: "The Endless Voyage" is the title of the De Chirico which had influenced him while young, and the background architecture is the Avery Court at the Wadsworth Atheneum. On either side of the central panel of this work, Coyer put a painting of flowers, in keeping with their history both as traditional offerings to the dead and as a metaphor for death, as in seventeenth century Dutch painting.

The flowers of the altarpiece lead into Coyer's most recent series of works: paintings based upon still lifes of flowers. Coyer had explored other genres; this one is a dangerous subject for a contemporary artist to handle, for it immediately opens him to charges of inconsequentiality and pandering to popular taste. This is not something new; it has been noted how the academic tradition ranked still life painting as the lowest form of painting, as the artist was "merely" copying what he saw before him. Flowers have also been the traditional subject of the Sunday painter. In our century, O'Keeffe has invigorated the subject, and the power of the academy has been swept away, but a suspicion persists on the part of the serious art world.

Coyer's floral works, however, are art about art. The subject of the paintings are not flowers painted from life. Instead, the artist has drawn on models from seventeenth century Dutch painters to the American Impressionist Frank Benson. Coyer takes vases and other vessels from those paintings; the flowers

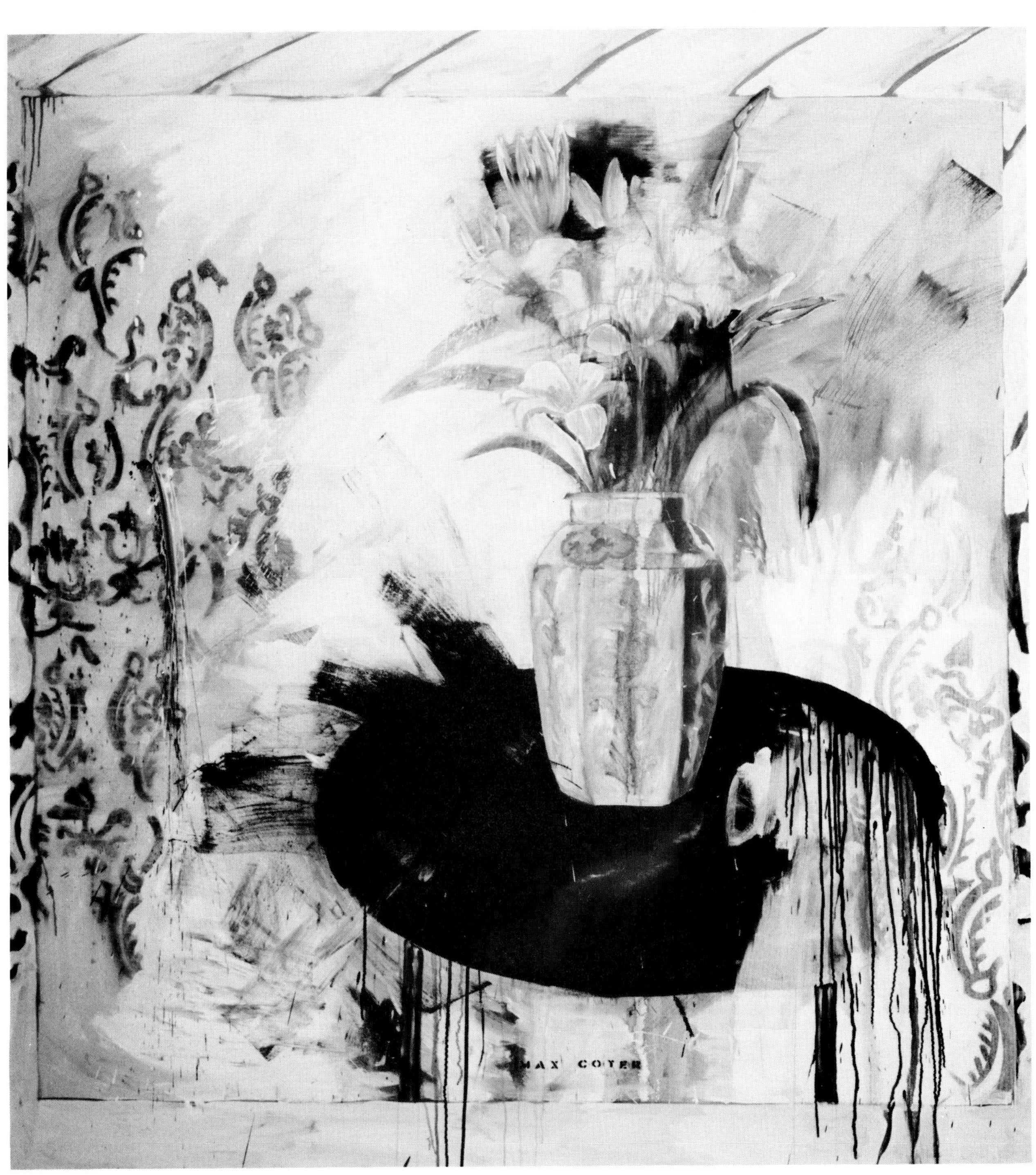


*Tiber*, 1987, oil on canvas, 78 x 84". Courtesy Gruenebaum Gallery, New York City.

themselves are usually drawn from photographs of flowers. The paintings are a paean not to nature but to the artist's recreation of nature in art.

The works are beautiful, but certainly not in a conventional fashion. Coyer scrapes away, overpaints, and otherwise alters his first strokes. Many of the works have the floral container set atop a round table, whose plane is set on a different perspective than the container's perspective. The round table's upper rim set off against the central floral piece is reminiscent of Coyer's earlier Conehead series, something he did not set out to do when he began the series, but it is obviously a form to which he is drawn. In other paintings, the flowers are juxtaposed with Frank Lloyd Wright's architecture, particularly "Falling Water." That house was Wright's most famous attempt to have a building situated harmoniously within its environment. For Coyer, however, the building has always seemed an ambitious failure; the technology of 1936 was insufficient to handle the stresses put on the cantilevers by gravity and the problems of humidity from the stream over which the house rests. The building is not one with nature, but rather one against nature. Coyer uses it in the floral works as an emblem of the artist's impulse to bend nature to his aesthetic impulse. The irony here, of which Coyer is fully aware, is that the "nature" to which Wright's architecture is here contrasted is not taken directly from life but is rather Coyer's own interpretation of an earlier interpretation of nature.

In the past seven years, Coyer has created an impressive body of work. Ambitious and prolific, he has succeeded in creating works which are both beautiful and intellectual. His images, no matter how sensuously presented (and Coyer's handling of paint is masterful), are always informed with the weight of art history. He mines the past lavishly, but he is not a mere copyist. As George Santisbury once wrote, "The charge of plagiarism is usually an excessively idle one; for when a man steals without genius, the thefts are mere fairy gold which turns to leaves and pebbles under his hand."[7] Whether or not Coyer's work is touched with genius must be left for future generations to decide, but for me his works always delight and instruct. Certainly they seem to indicate one of the few viable strategies for a painter in the last quarter of the twentieth century. Postmodern art has been criticized for promoting a kind of stylish eclecticism, everything by turns and nothing long. At its best, however, such a program may approach a "game" that Hermann Hesse envisaged being played by the intellectuals of a future world:

> One theme, two themes, or three themes were stated, elaborated, varied, and underwent a development quite similar to that of the theme in a Bach fugue or a concerto movement. A Game, for example, might start from a given astronilmical configuration, or from the actual theme of a Bach fugue, or from a sentence out of Leibniz or the Upanishads, and from this theme, depending on the intentions and talents of the player, it could either further explore and elaborate the initial motif or else enrich its expressiveness by allusions to kindred concepts.[8]

Coyer, in his chosen art, shows every evidence of acquiring a mastery of the Glass Bead Game. Keep playing, Max.

REAGAN UPSHAW

[1]For this and the two quotations immediately following, see Judy K. Collischan Van Wagner, "A Radical Idea: An Interview with Max Coyer," *Arts Magazine,* Vol. 59, No. 1 (September, 1984), p. 112. Other quotes from Max Coyer not specifically cited are from the artist's conversations with Reagan Upshaw, June-July, 1987.

[2]*Ibid,* p. 112.

[3]*Ibid,* p. 112.

[4]*ibid,* p. 112.

[5]Yet in using both Picasso and Ingres in similar fashion, Coyer was performing an act of synthesis, for as he wrote in 1984, "One must realize that the essence of French Painting circles around the image of woman as a type of stabilizing creature (note such artists as Ingres and David) and that Picasso's vision took an antithetical position to that tradition." Max Coyer, "Three Parts of a Movement," in Max Coyer. New Paintings (Chicago: Klein Gallery, 1984), n.p.

[6]Richard Martin, "Max Coyer," *Arts Magazine,* Vol. 60, No. 2 (October, 1985), p. 122.

[7]George Santisbury, Introduction to *Tristam Shandy* by Laurence Sterne (New York: Dutton, 1964), p. xx.

[8]Hermann Hesse, *Magister Ludi,* trans. Richard and Clara Winston (New York: Bantam Books, 1970), p. 30.

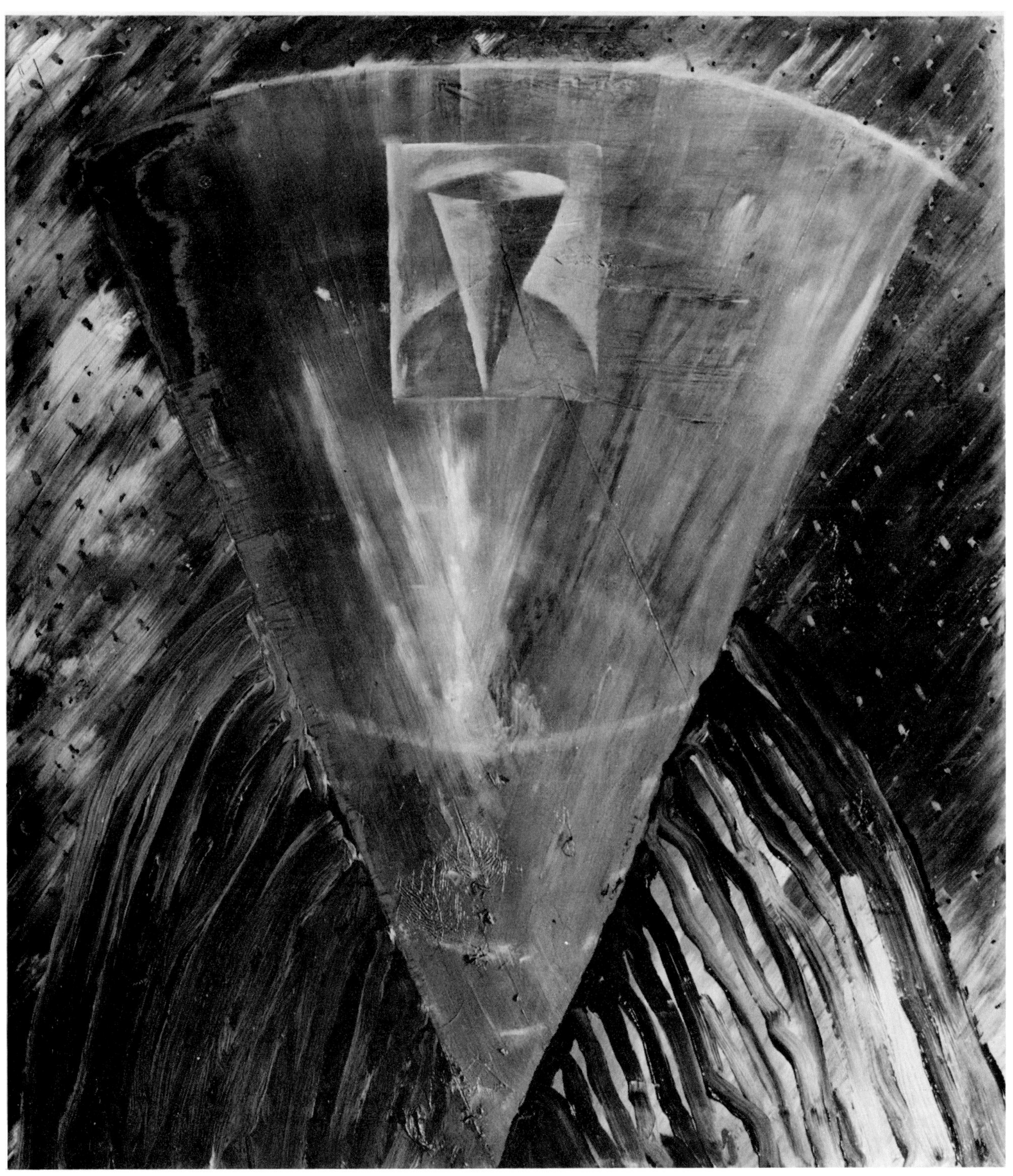

*Re-Entry,* 1983, oil on canvas, 46 x 40"

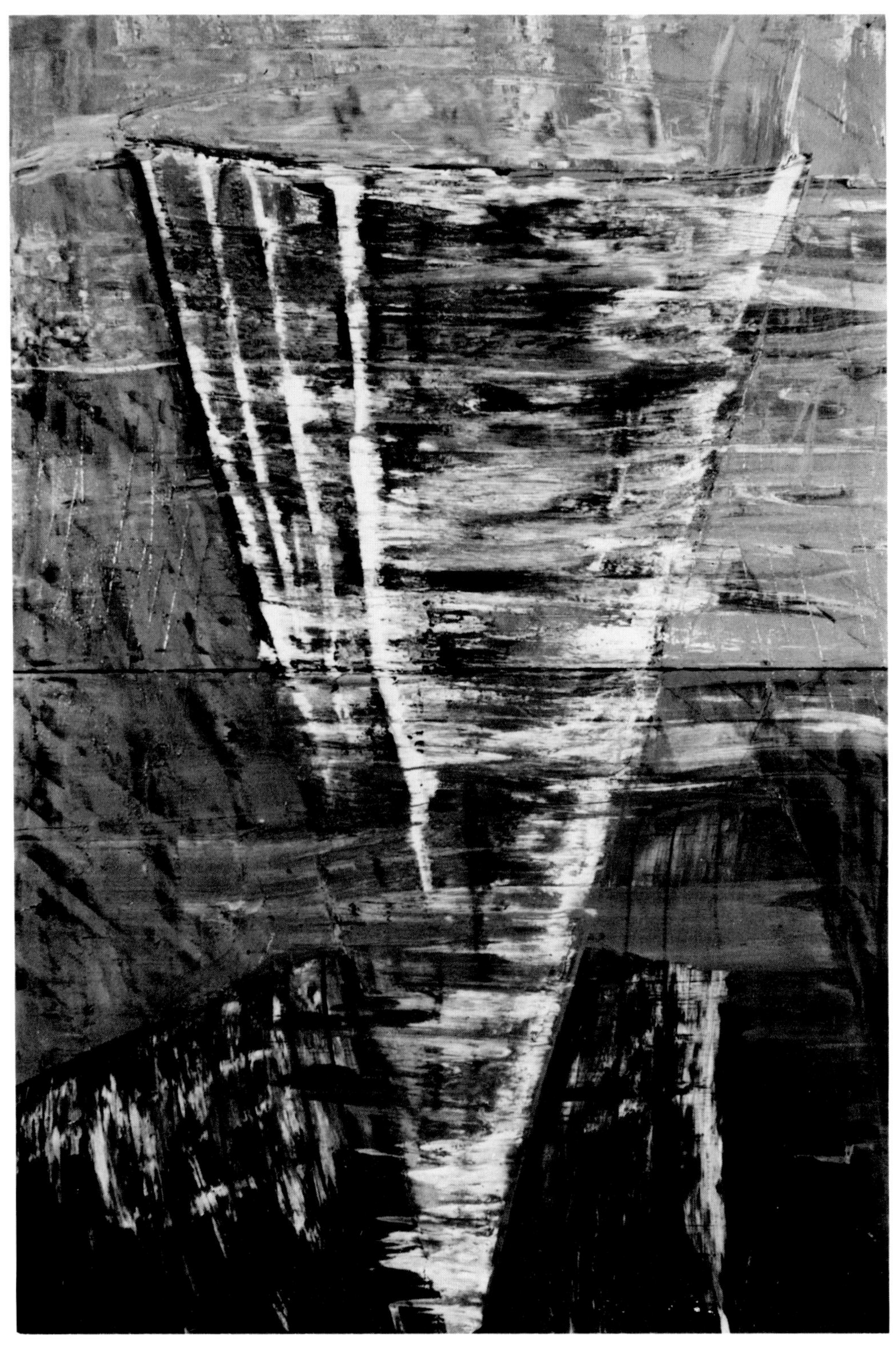

*Poikilothron,* 1983, oil on canvas, 60 x 40". Collection Mr. Edward Albee.

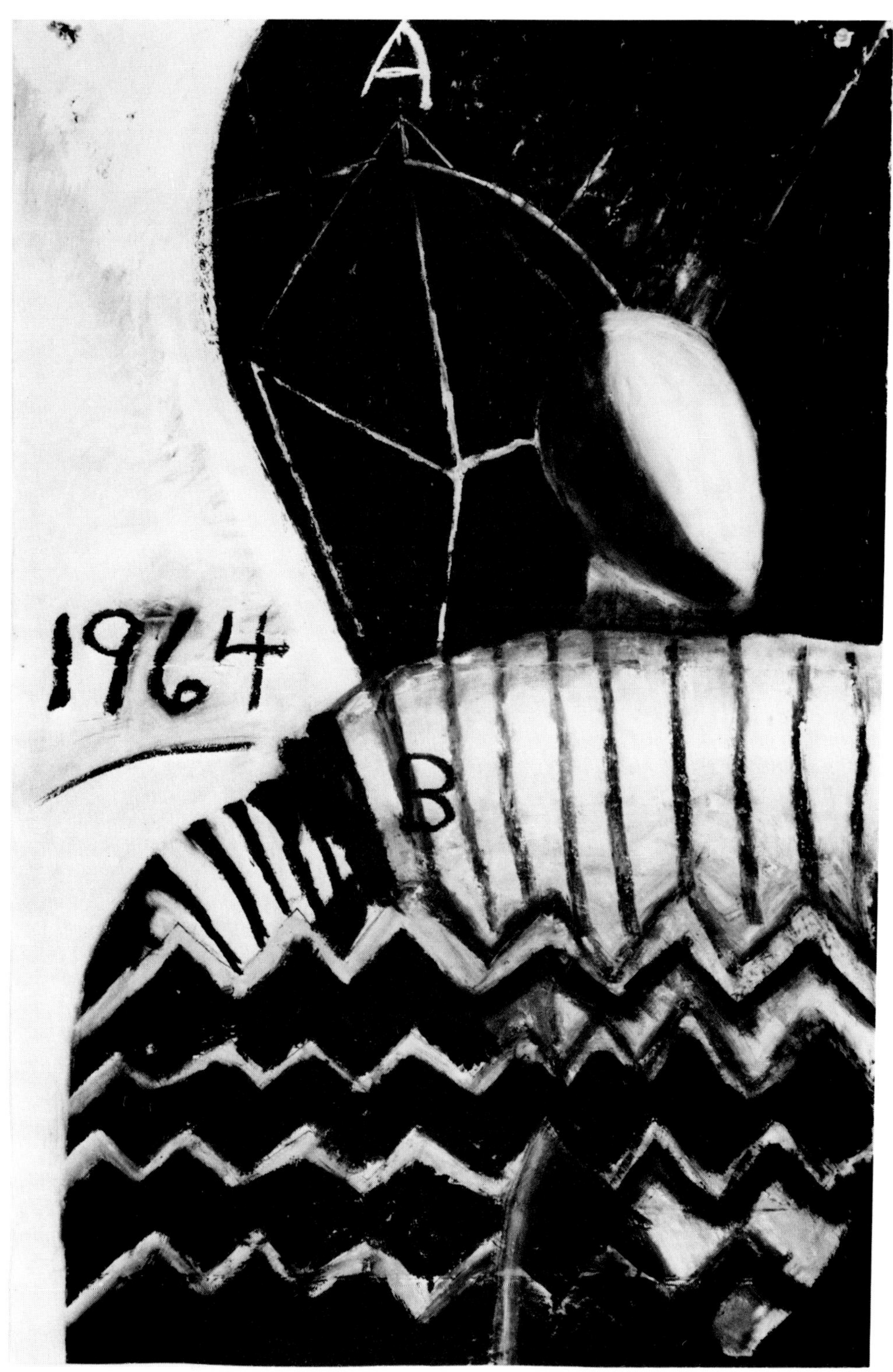


*1964-B*, 1983, oilstick and pastel on paper, 46 1/2 x 30".

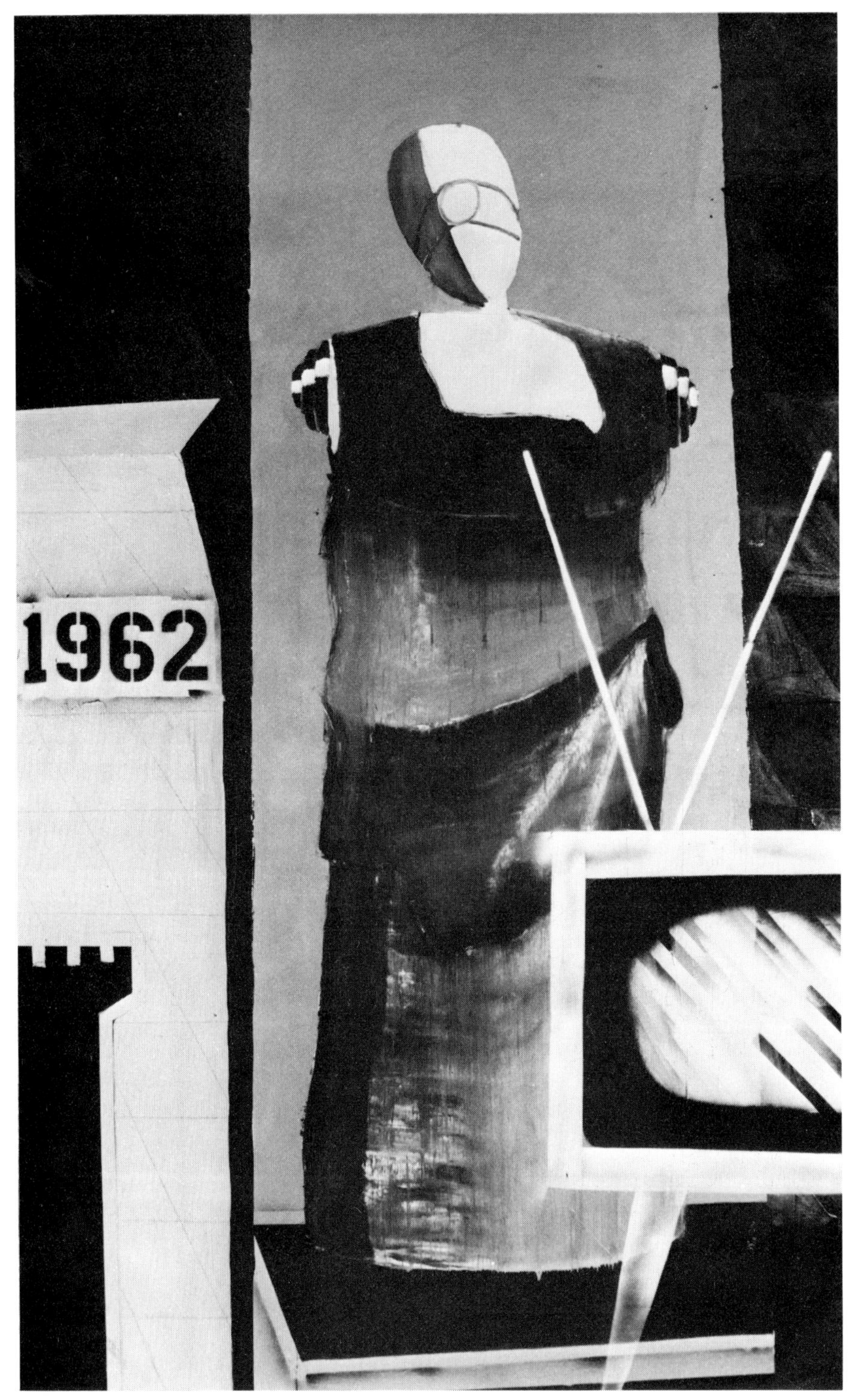



*The Endless Voyage*, 1983, oil on canvas with spray enamel, 82 x 48″

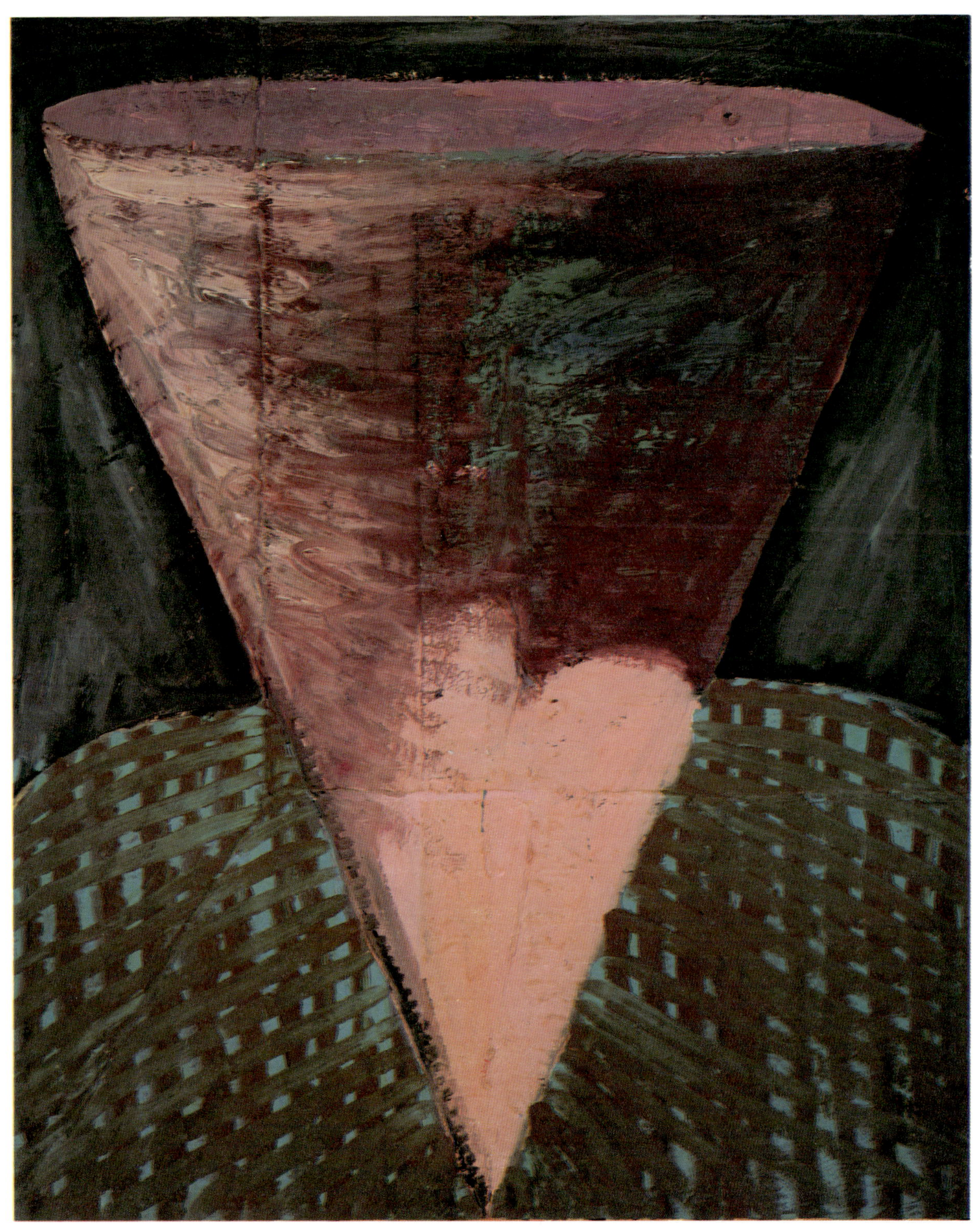

*Cranach the Elder Cone,* 1982, oil on canvas, 52 x 42".

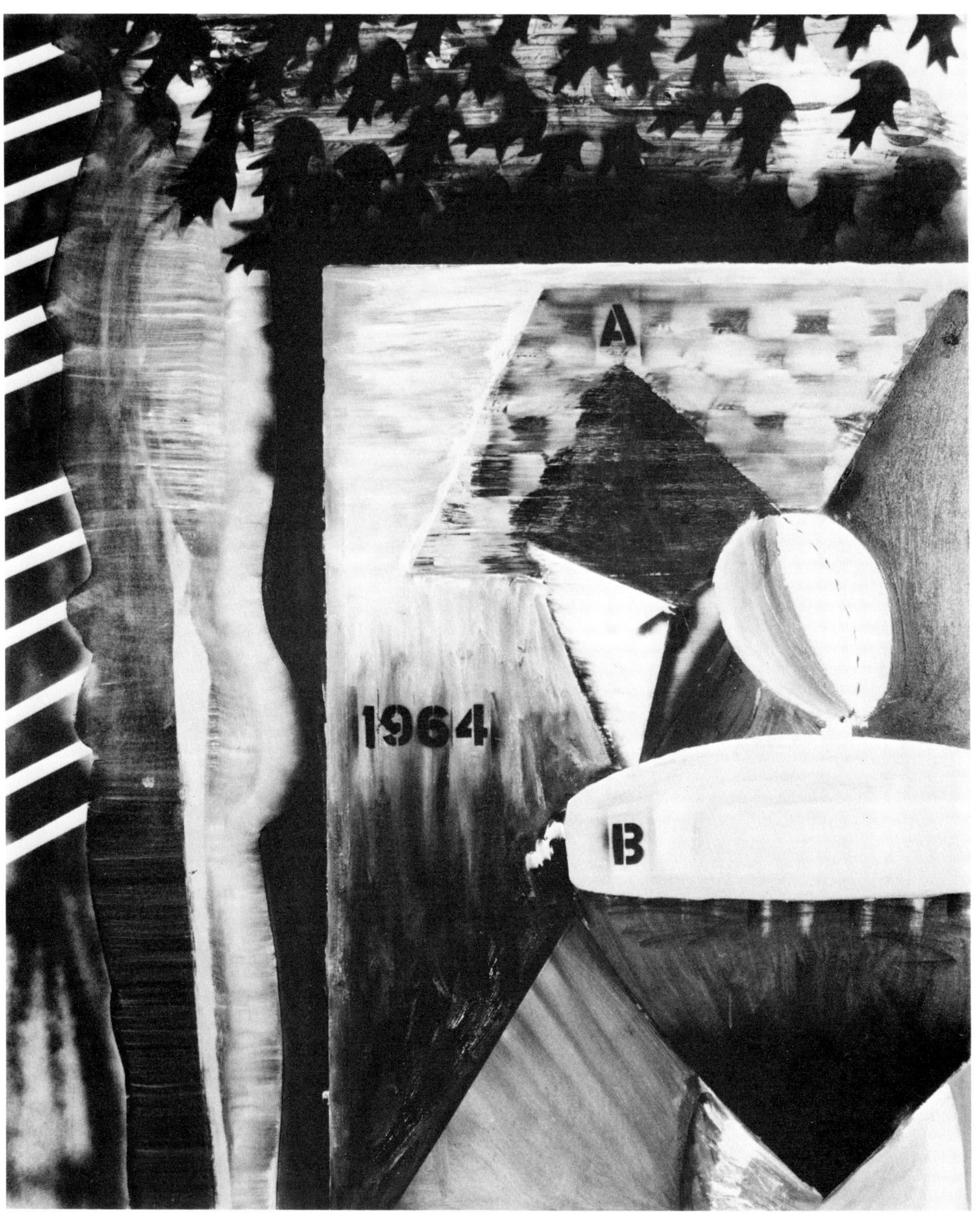

*1964-B,* 1983, oil on canvas with spray enamel, 60 x 48". Collection Mr. Harm Bouckaert.

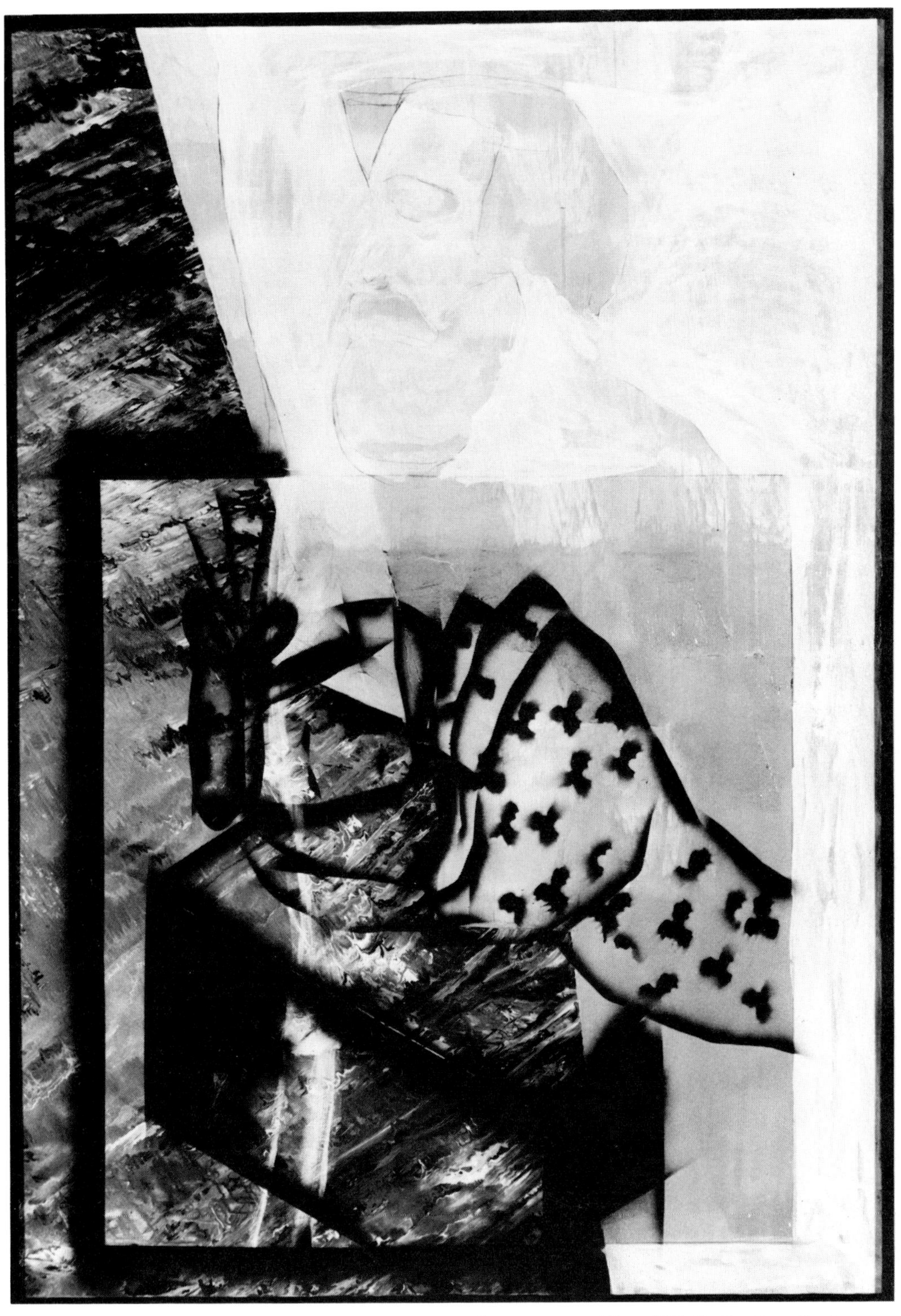

*Apparent Geisha,* 1984, oil and spray enamel on canvas, 70 x 48". Collection Best Products Inc.

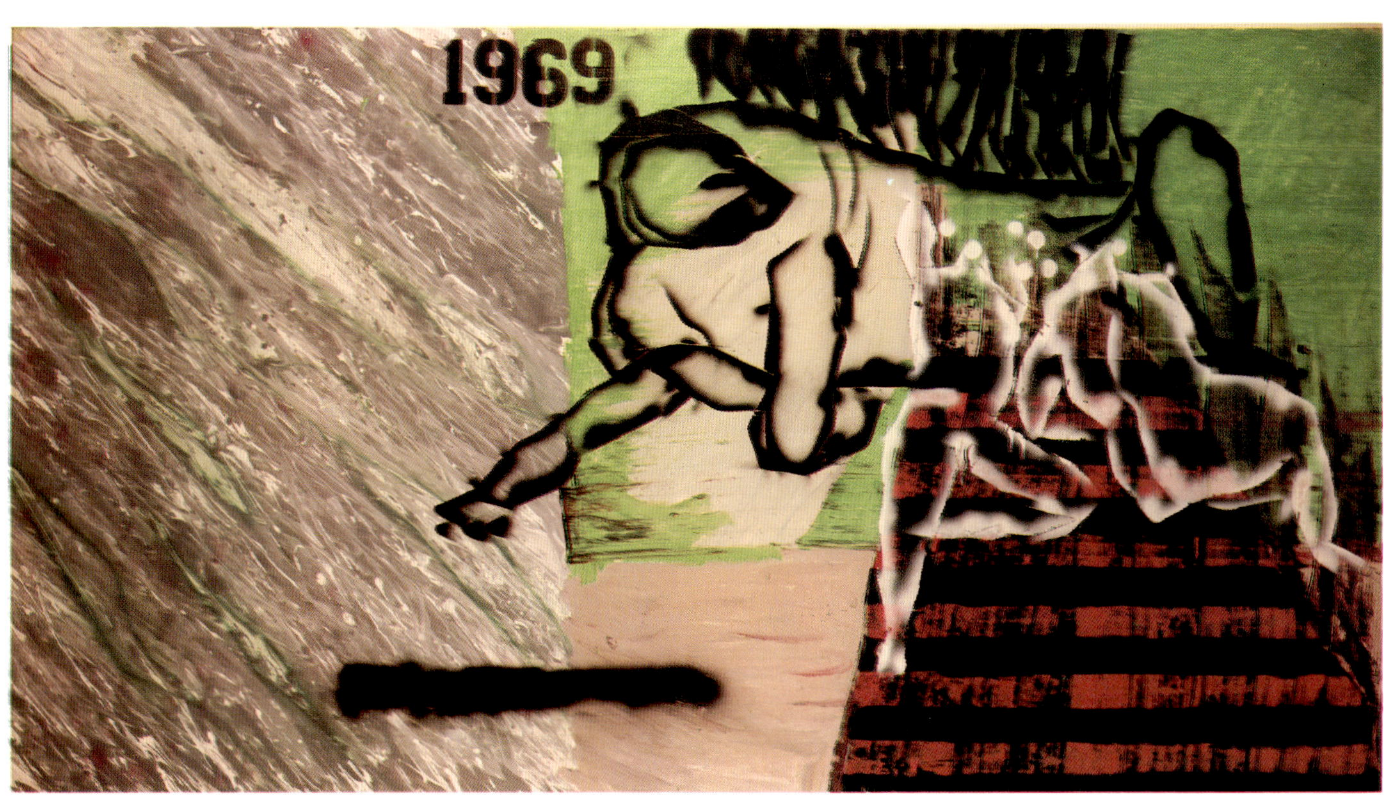



*La Lupa,* 1983, oil on canvas, 48 x 84".

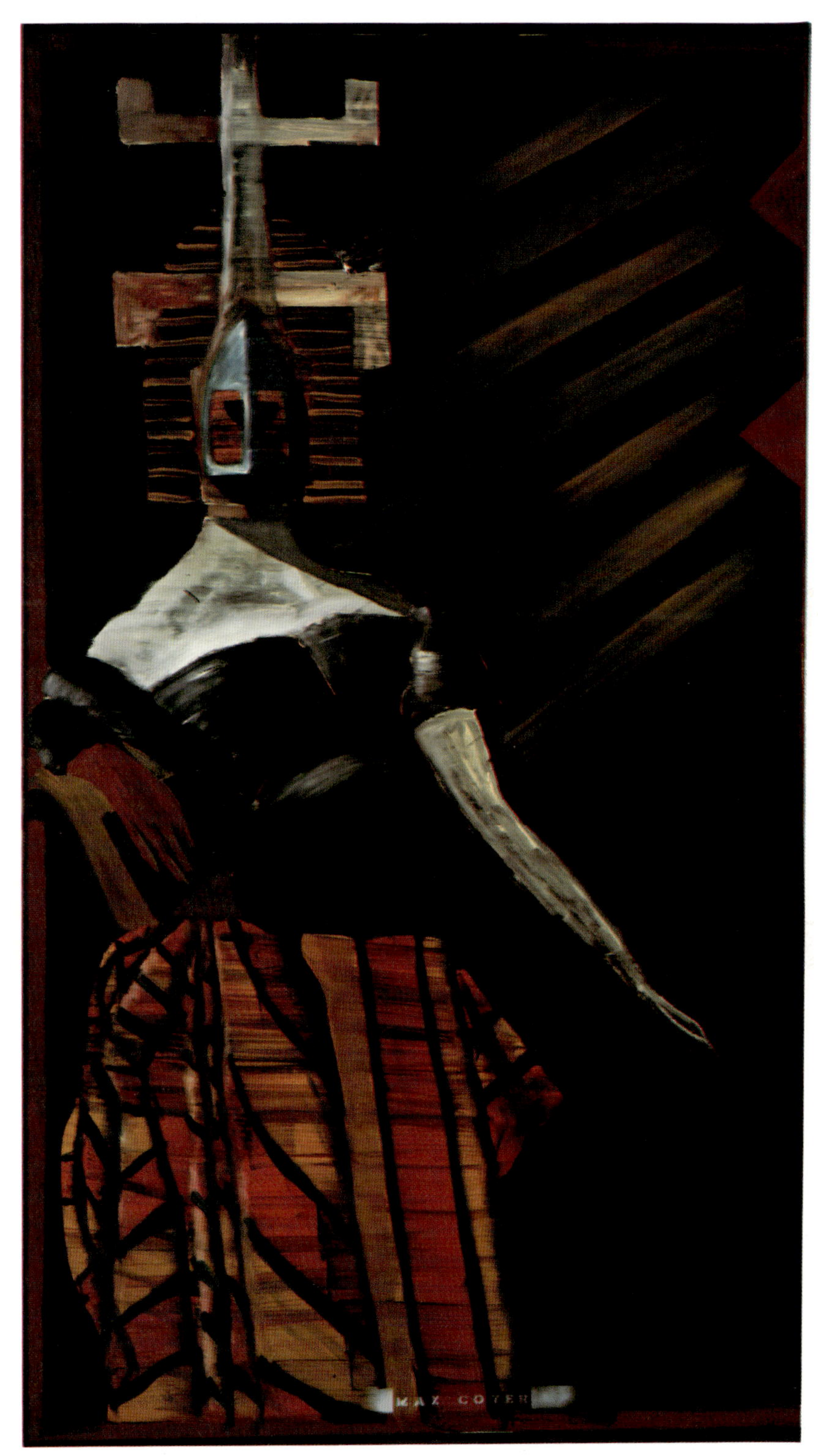

*The Beginning of the Apotheosis*, 1984, oil on canvas, 84 x 48".

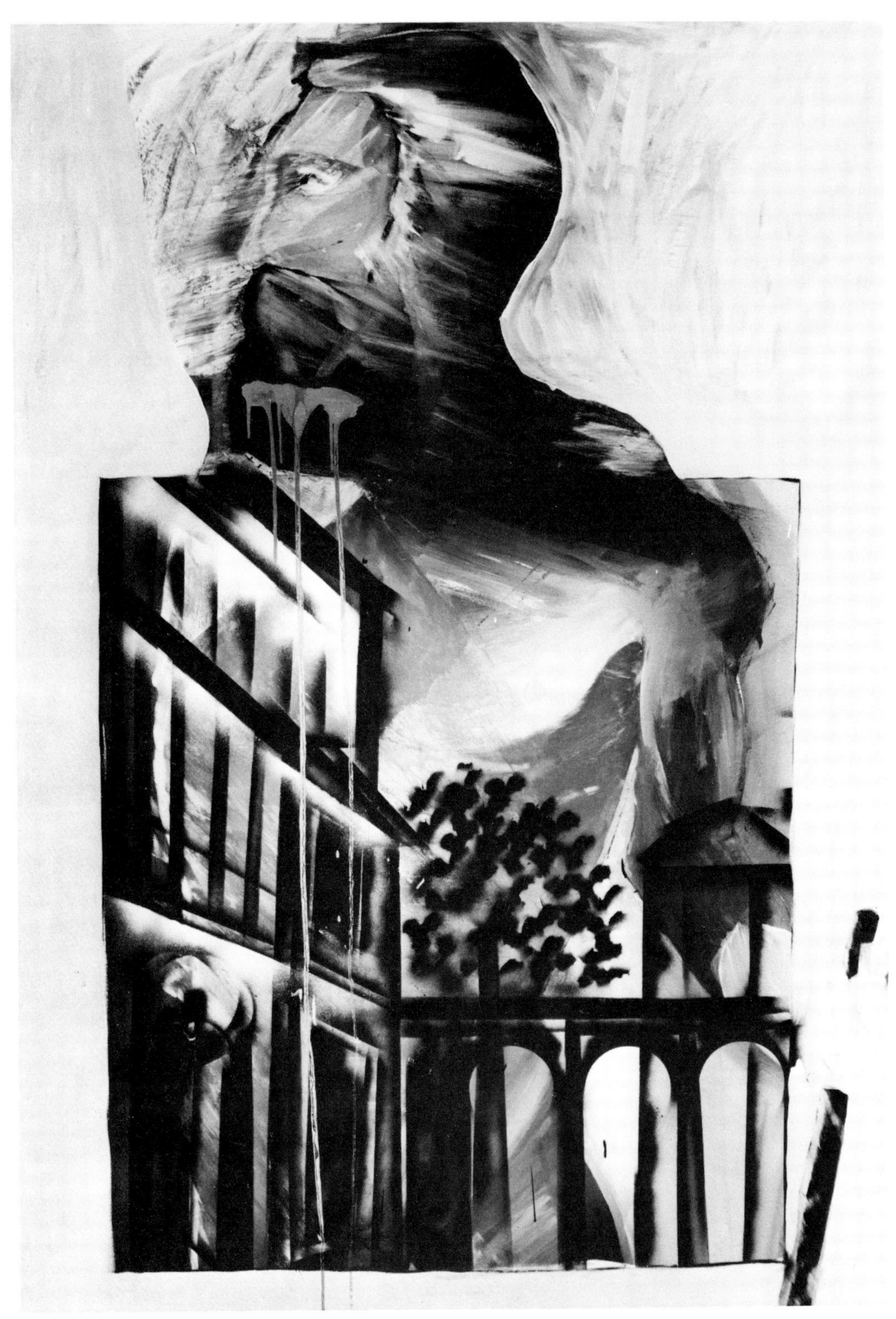

*Education,* 1984, oil and spray enamel on canvas, 70 x 48".

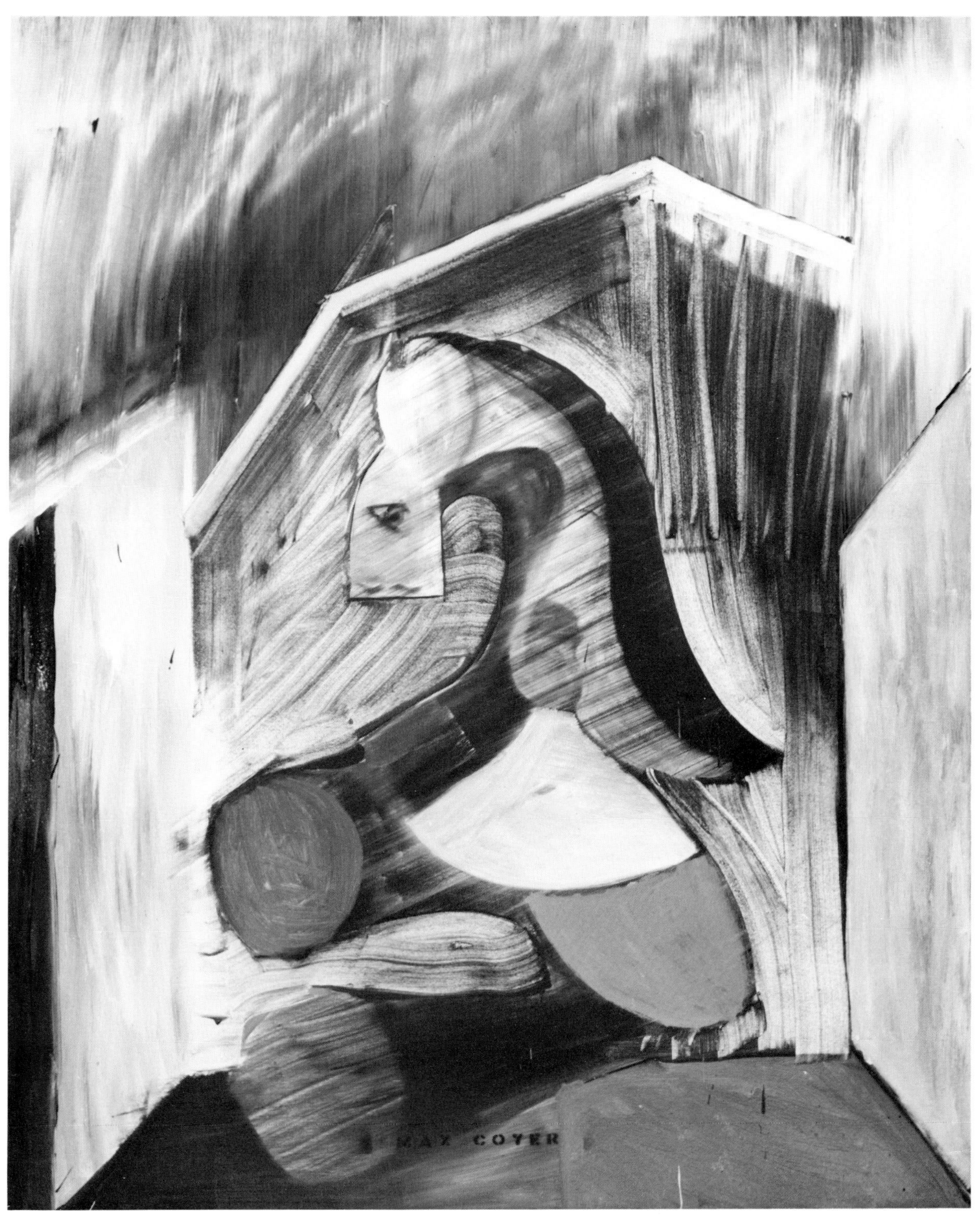



*Dora Maar*, 1984, oil on canvas, 60 x 48".

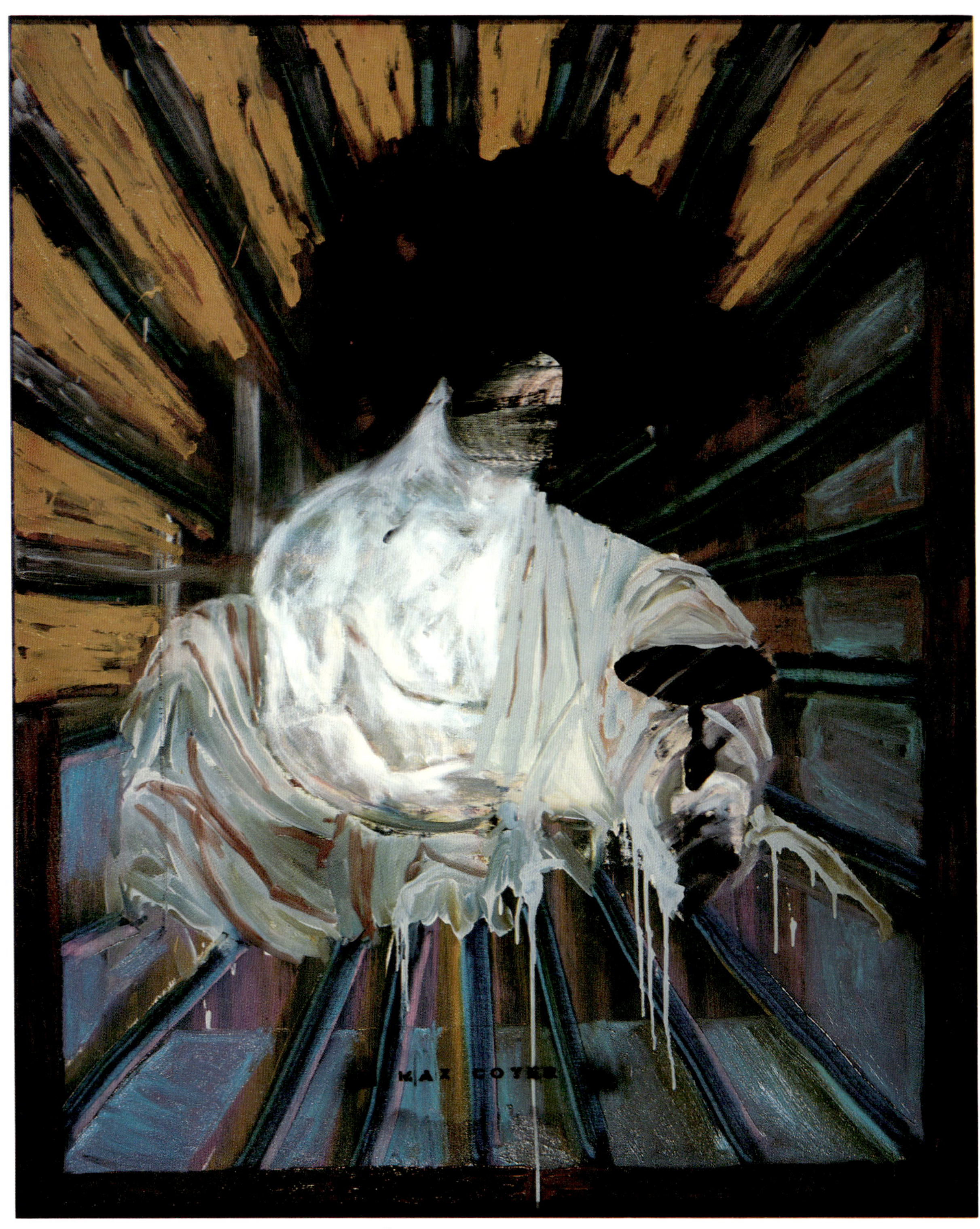

*Bacchus,* 1984, oil on canvas, 60 x 48".

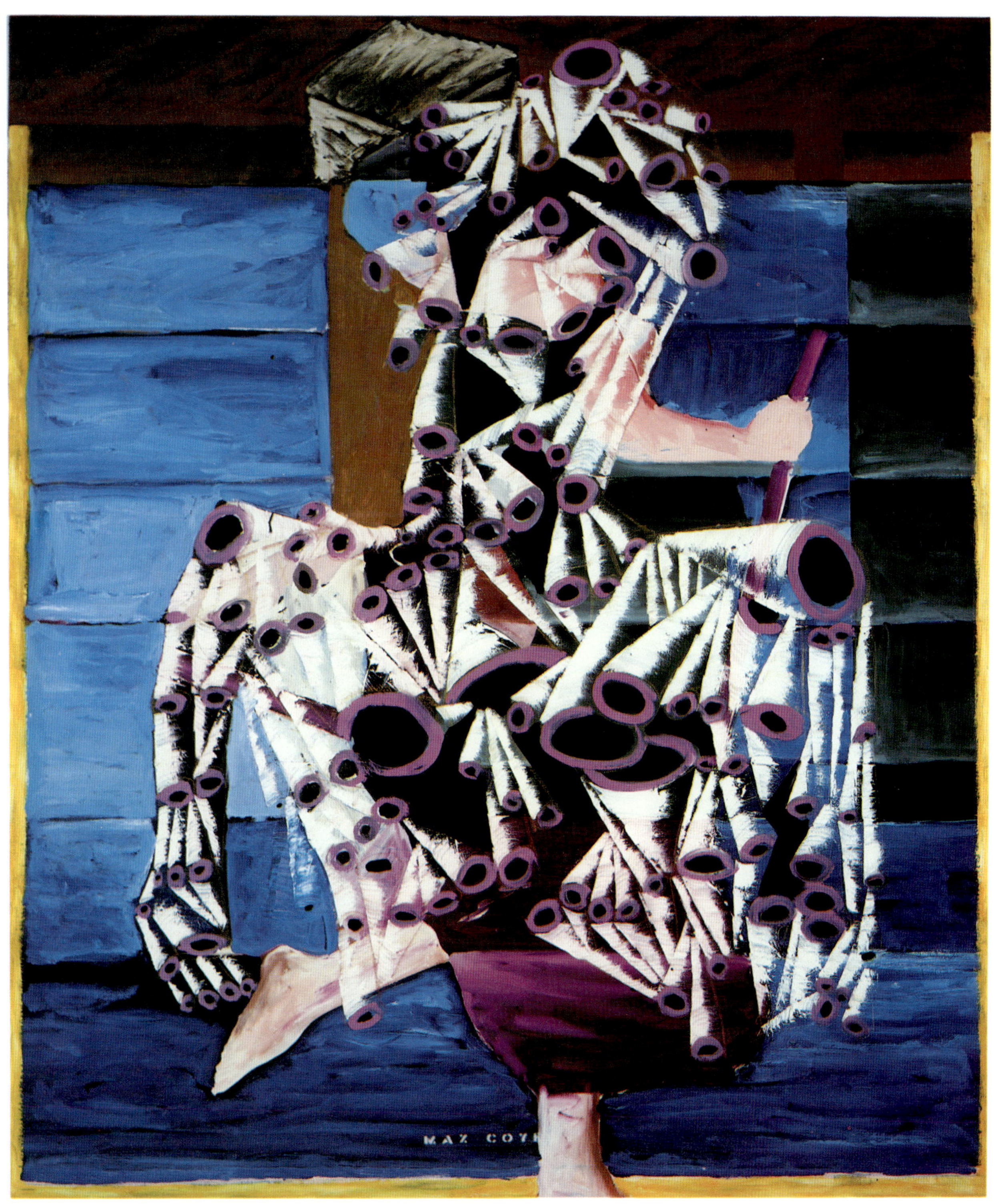



*Sacred Monster.* 1985, oil on canvas, 72 x 60".

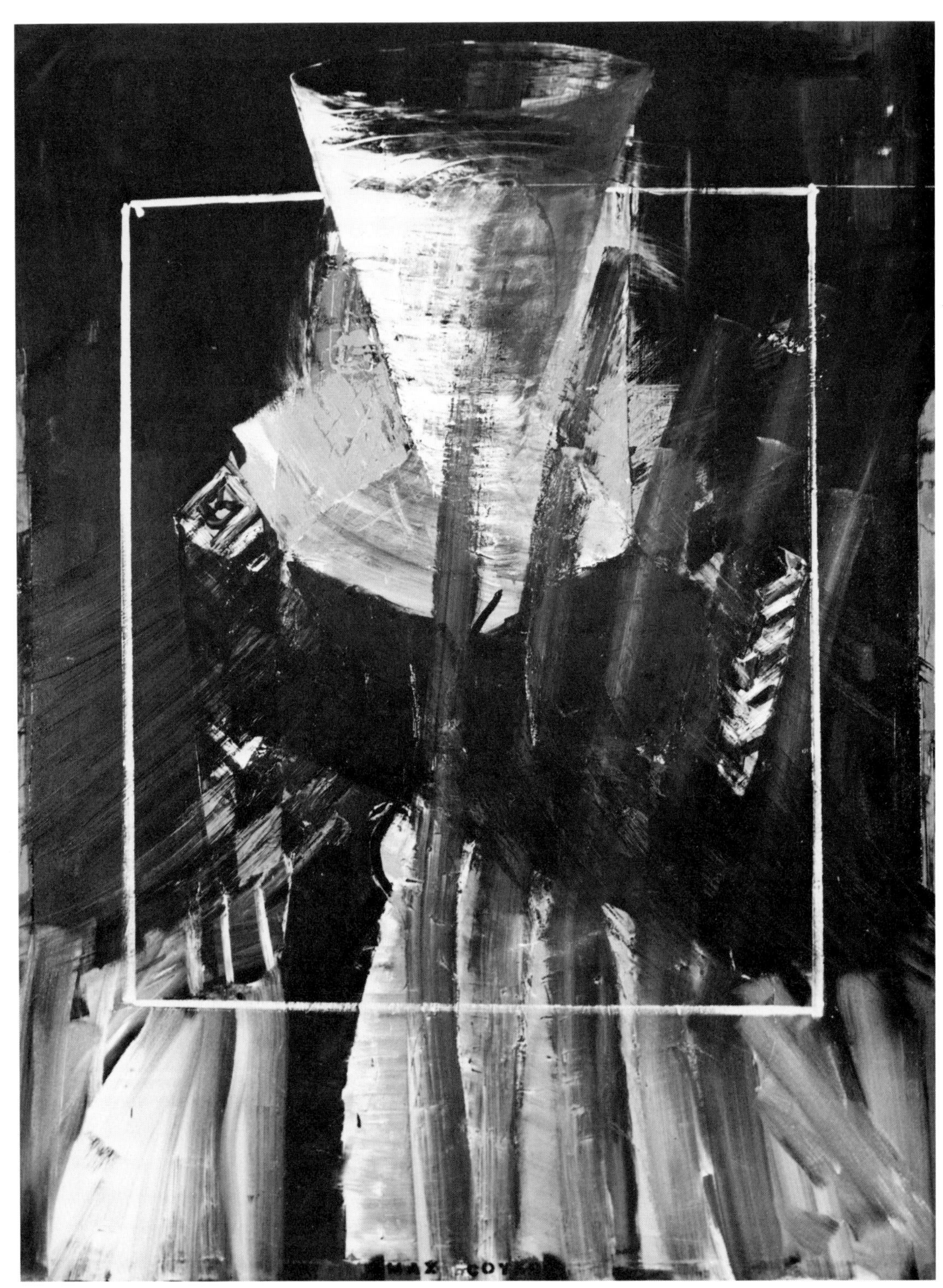

*Madame de Sade Conehead*, 1984, oil on canvas, 62 x 46". Collection Mr. & Mrs. Mark Taylor.

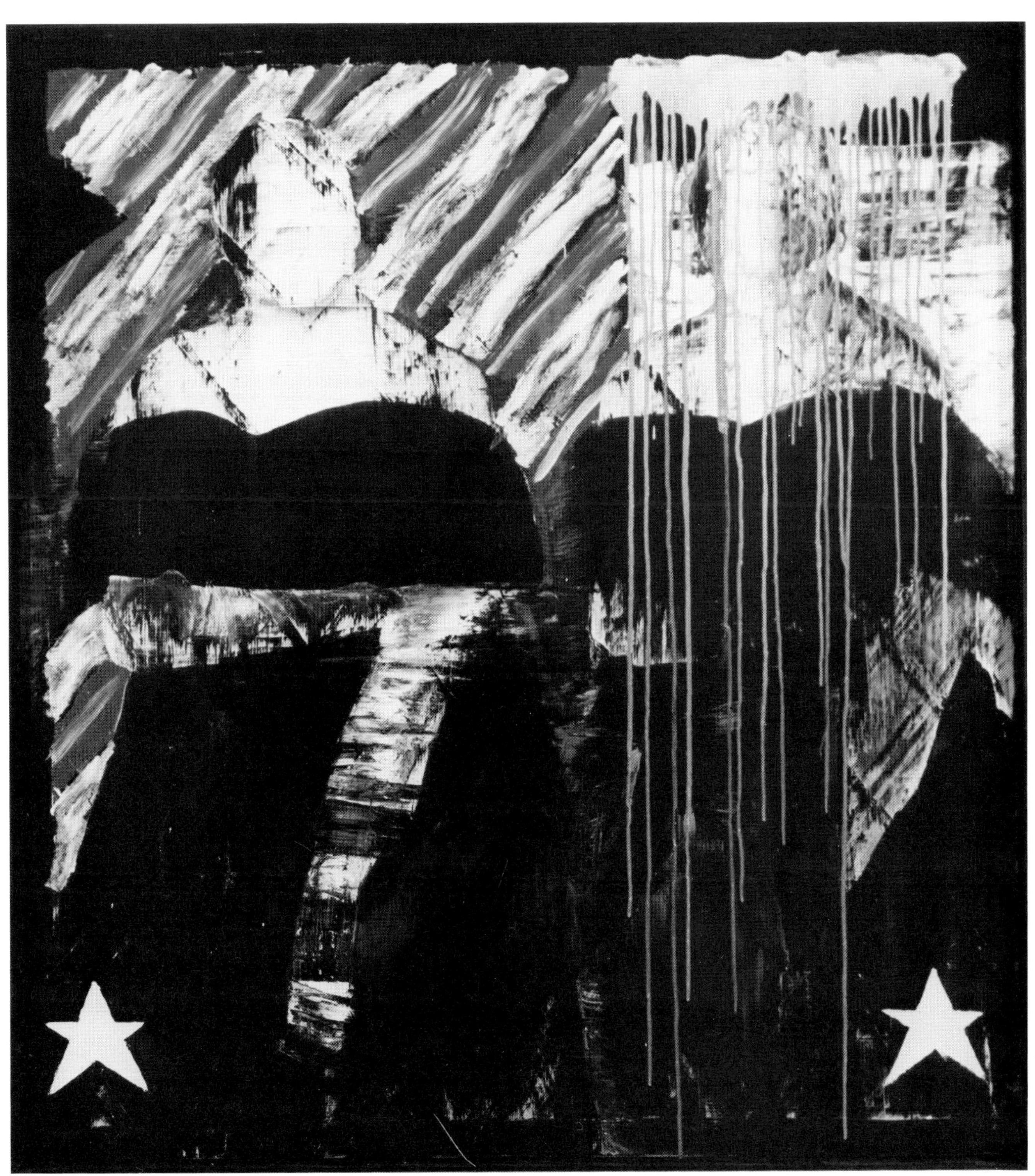

*Double Madame de Sade,* 1984, oil on canvas, 53 x 47″. Collection Mr. Sydney Singer.

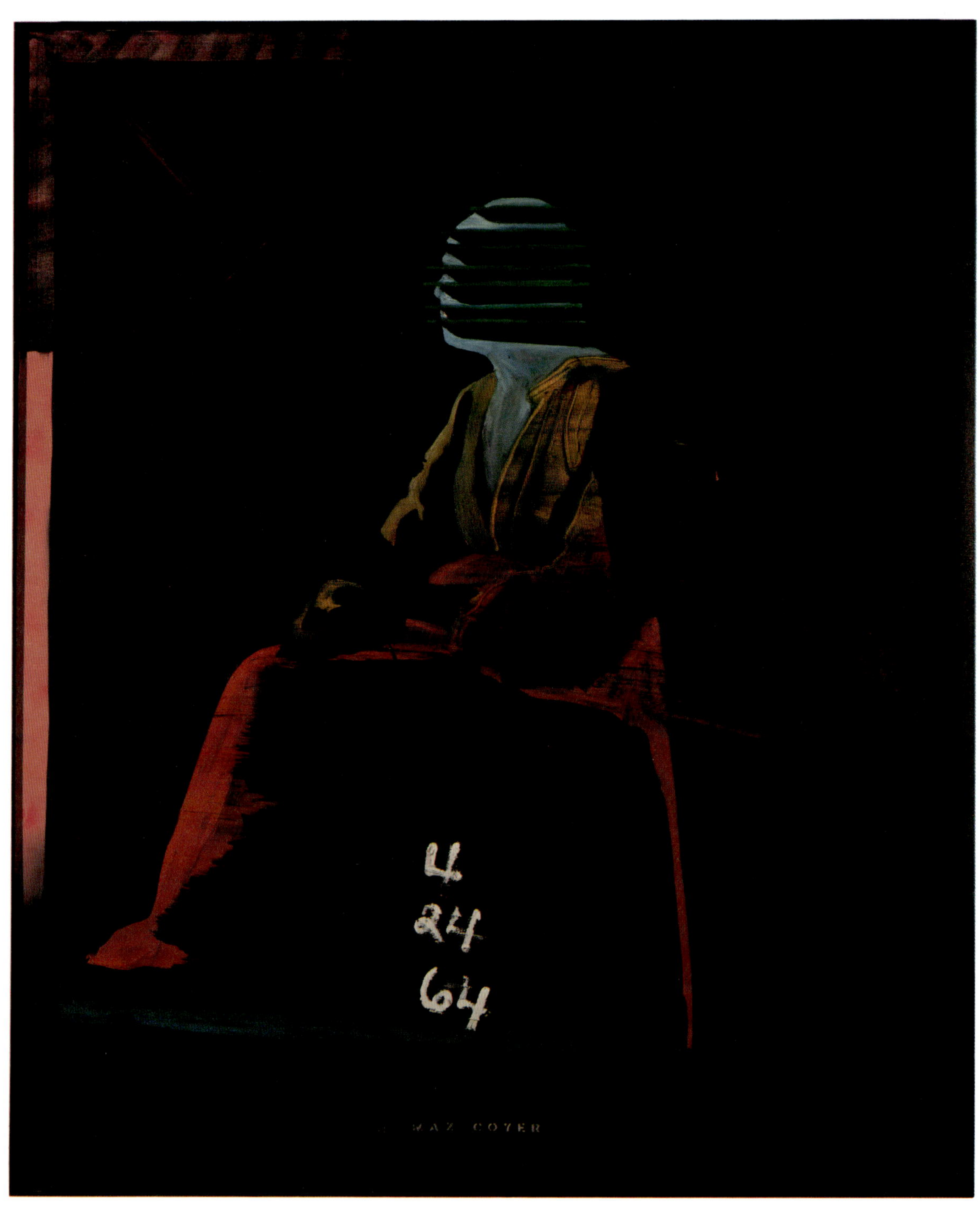

*The Hours,* 1985, oil on canvas, 72 x 60". Collection Mr. Michael Frey.

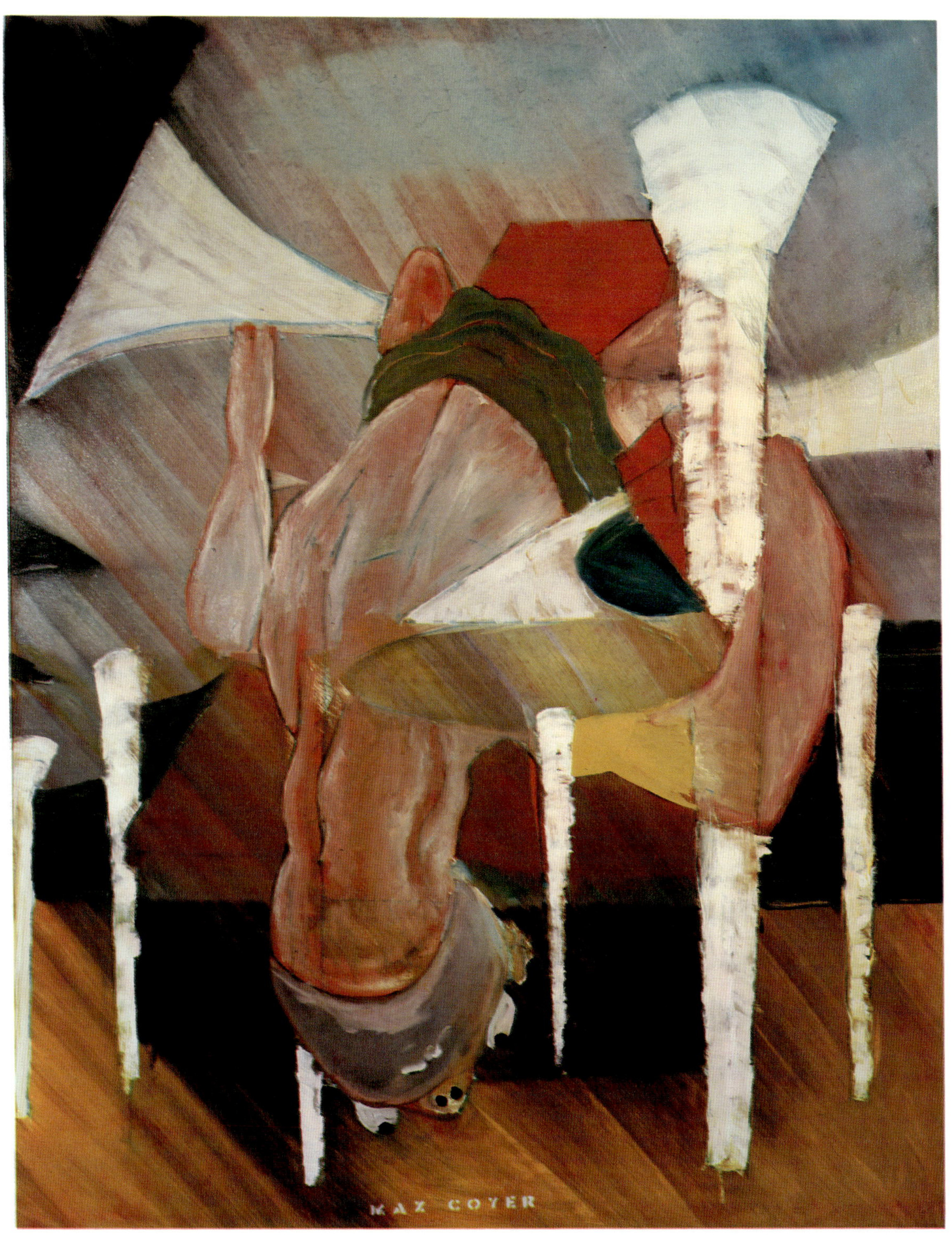



*Johnson's Wax*, 1985, oil on canvas, 60 x 46".

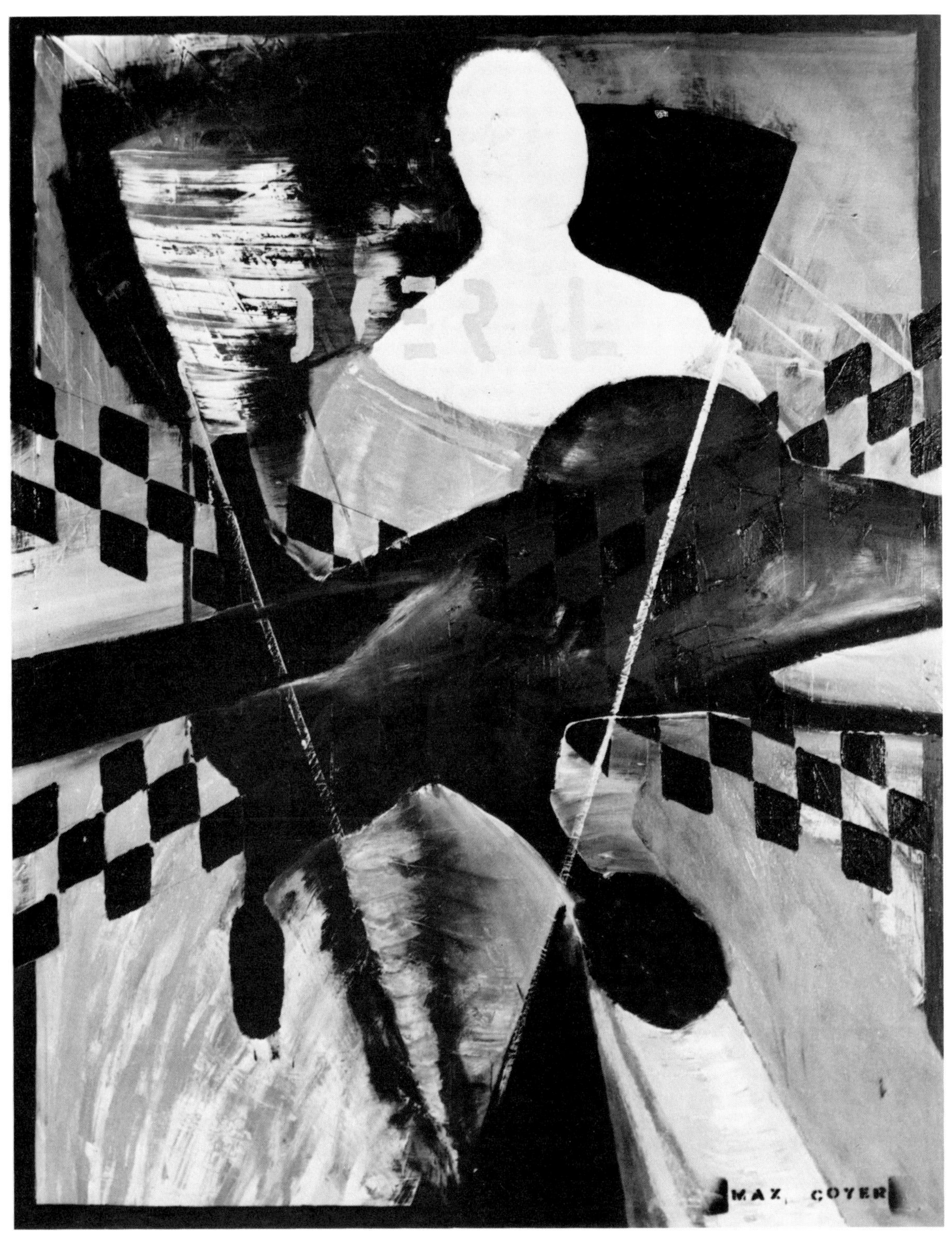


*Overal,* 1984, oil on canvas, 60 x 46".

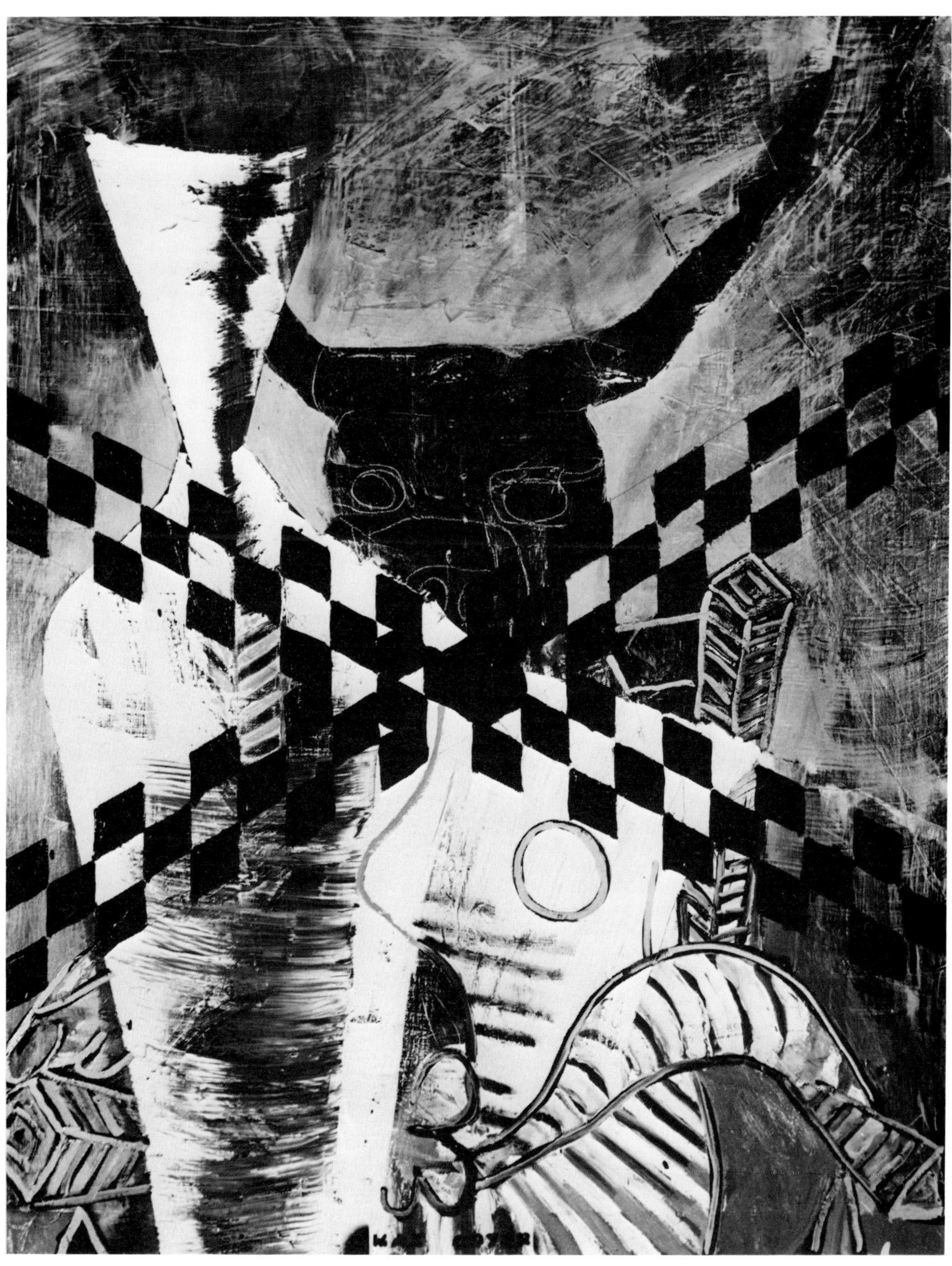

*Shaman*, 1984, oil on canvas, 60 x 46". Private Collection.

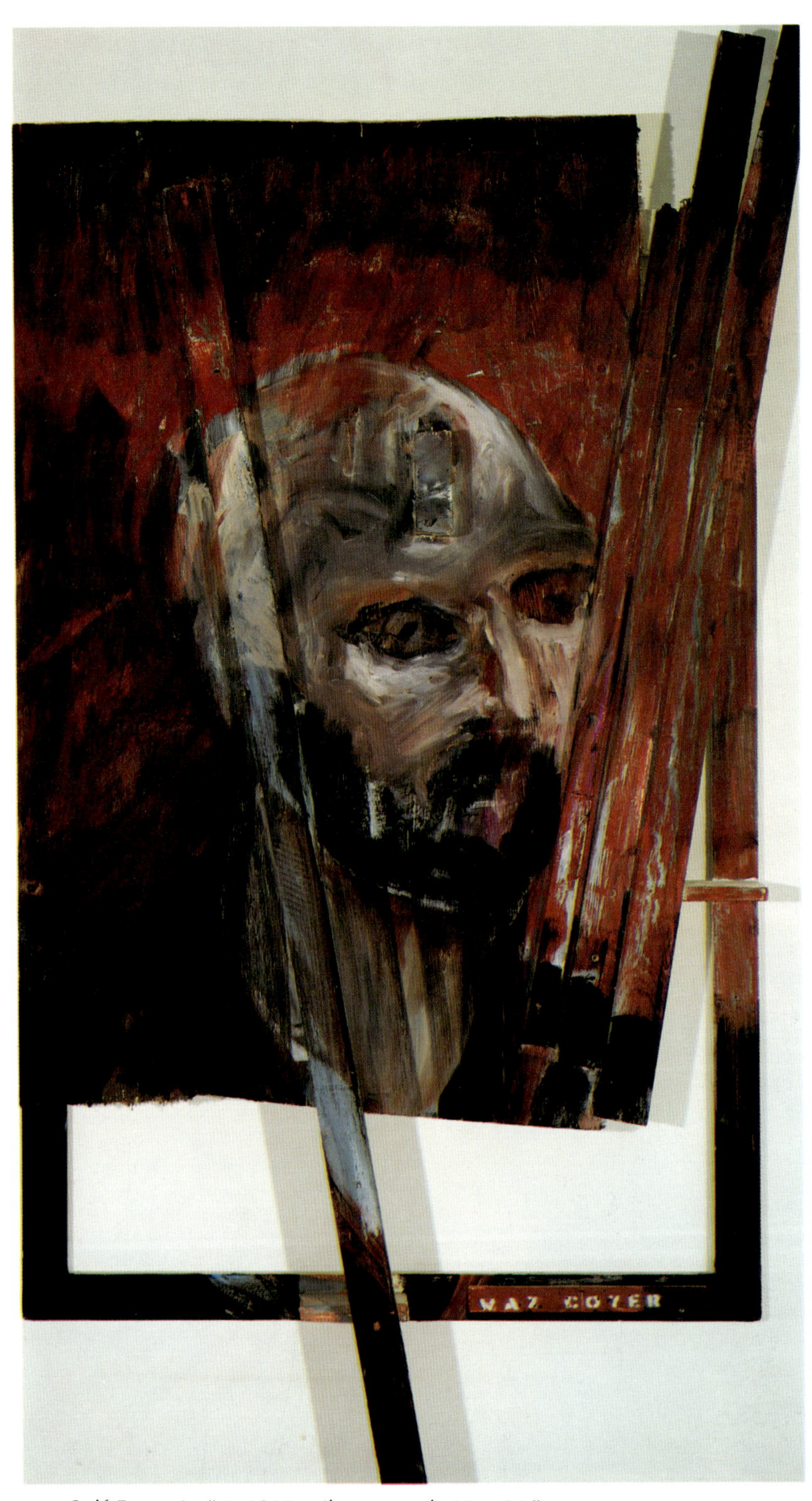


*Self-Portrait #4*, 1985, oil on wood, 65 x 35".

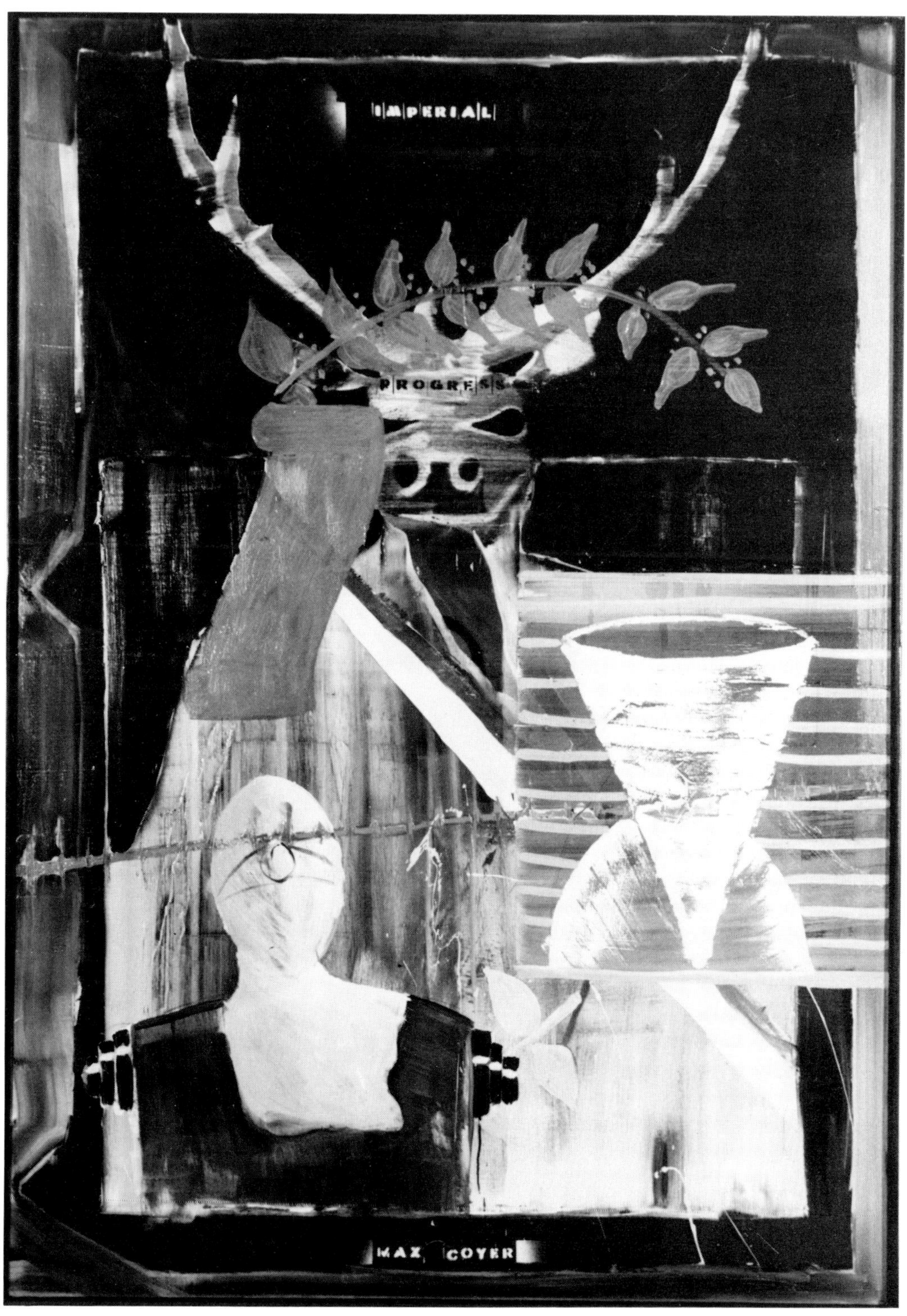


*Imperial Progress,* 1984, oil on canvas, 70 x 48″.

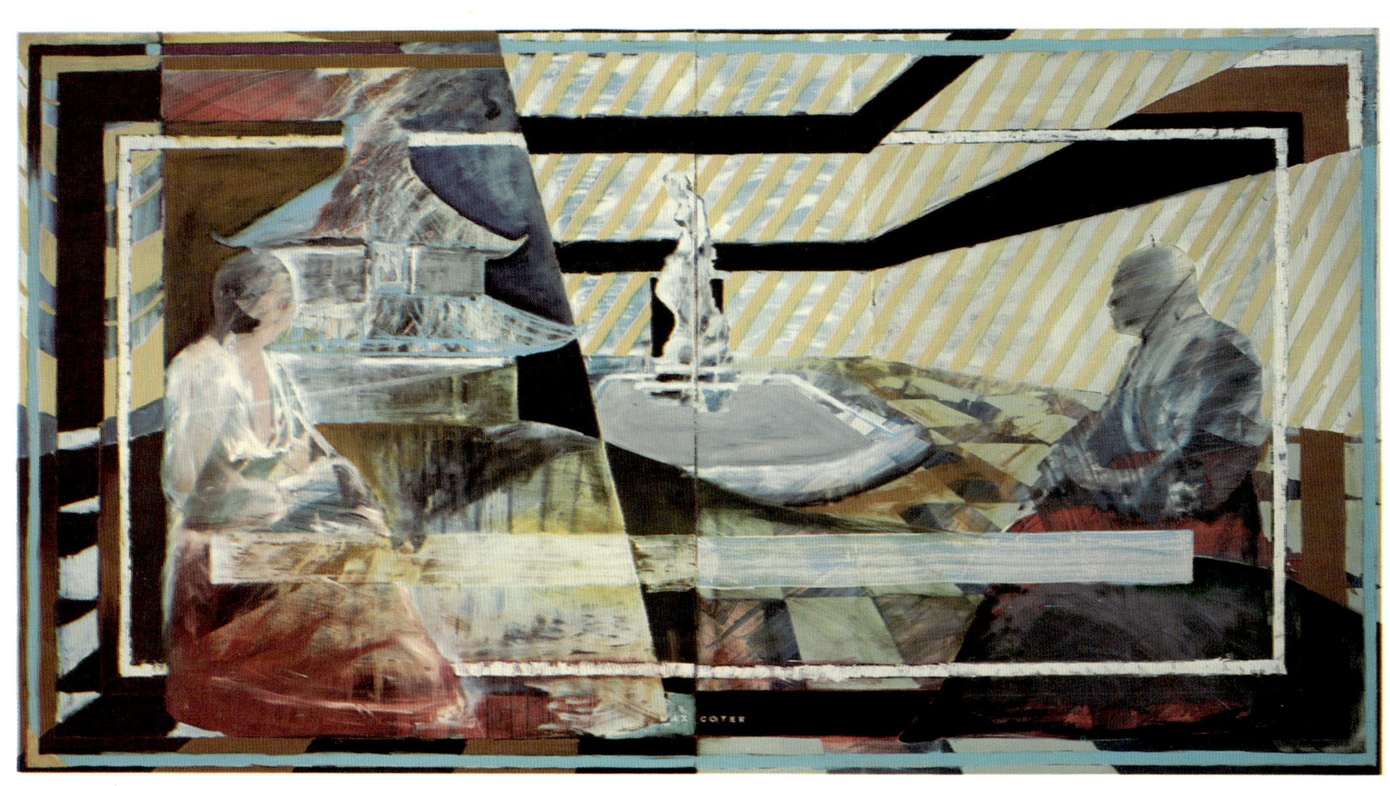

*The Endless Voyage*, 1986, oil on canvas, 76 x 144".

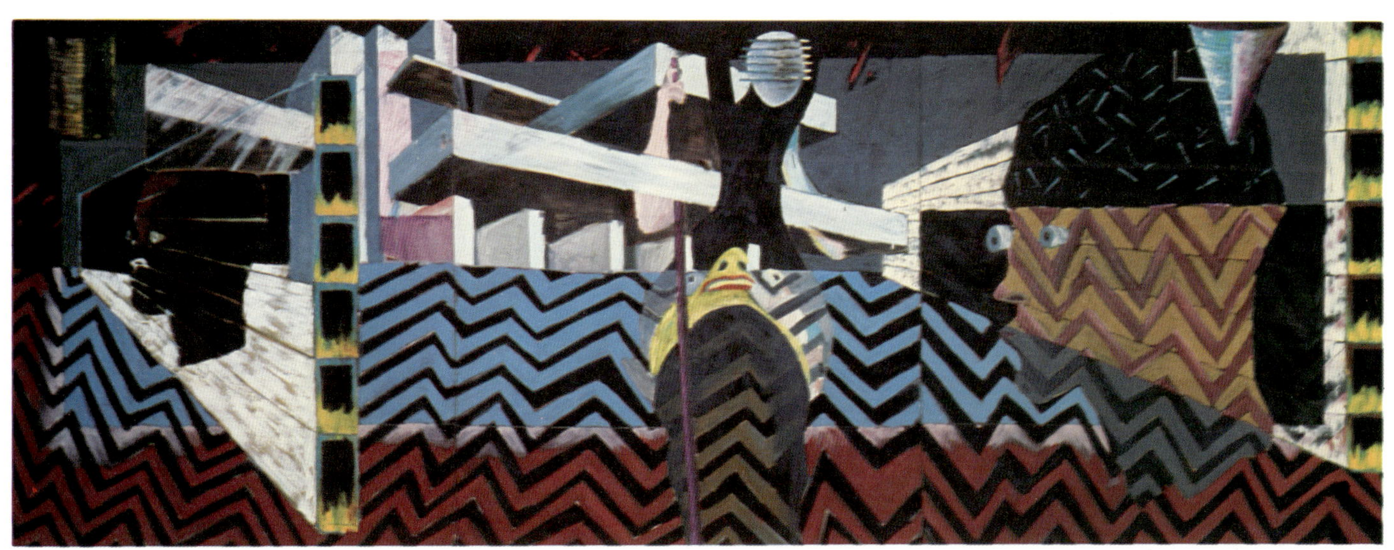

*Rising Water*, 1985, oil on canvas, 72 x 180".

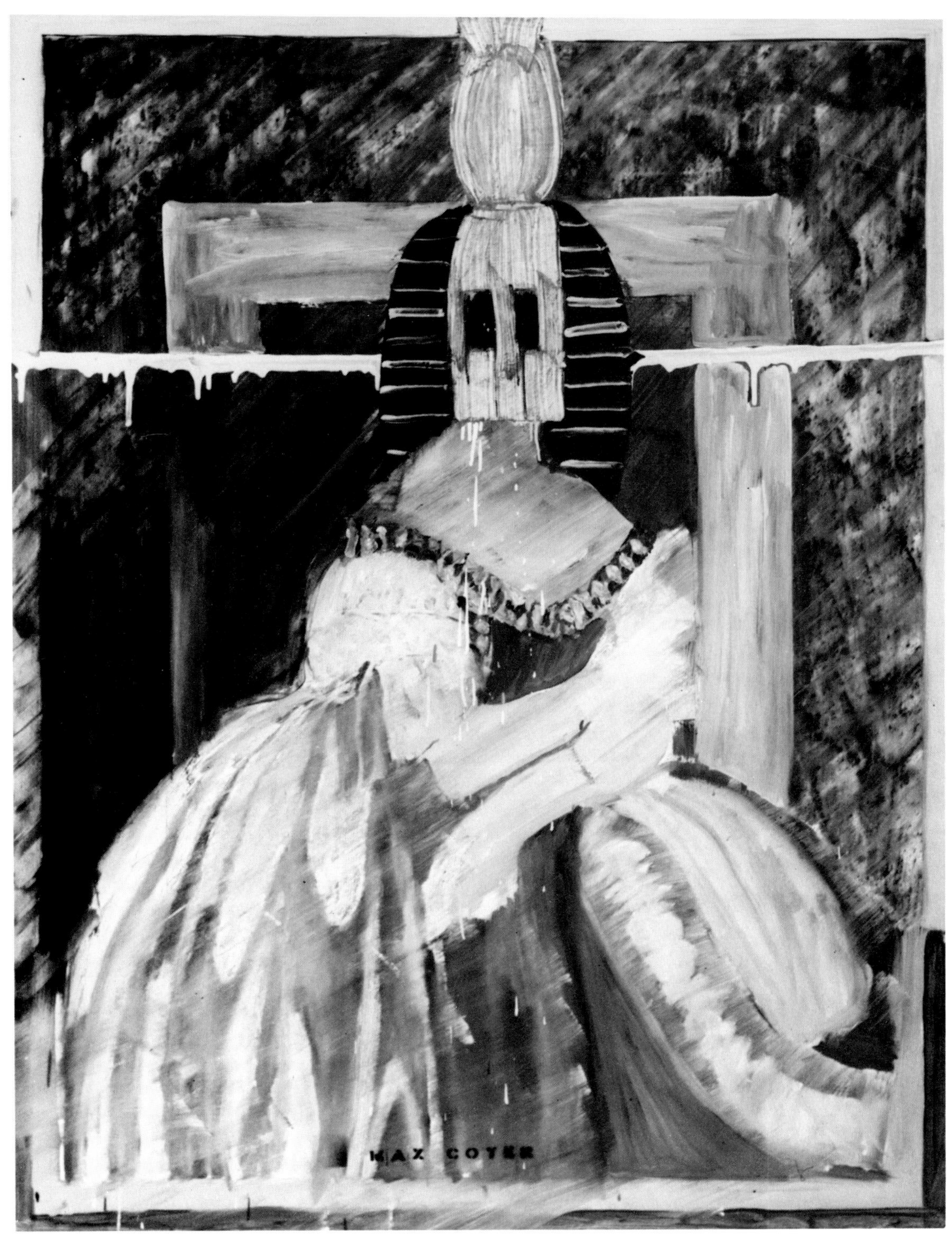



*The Hostess,* 1984, oil on canvas 60 x 48".

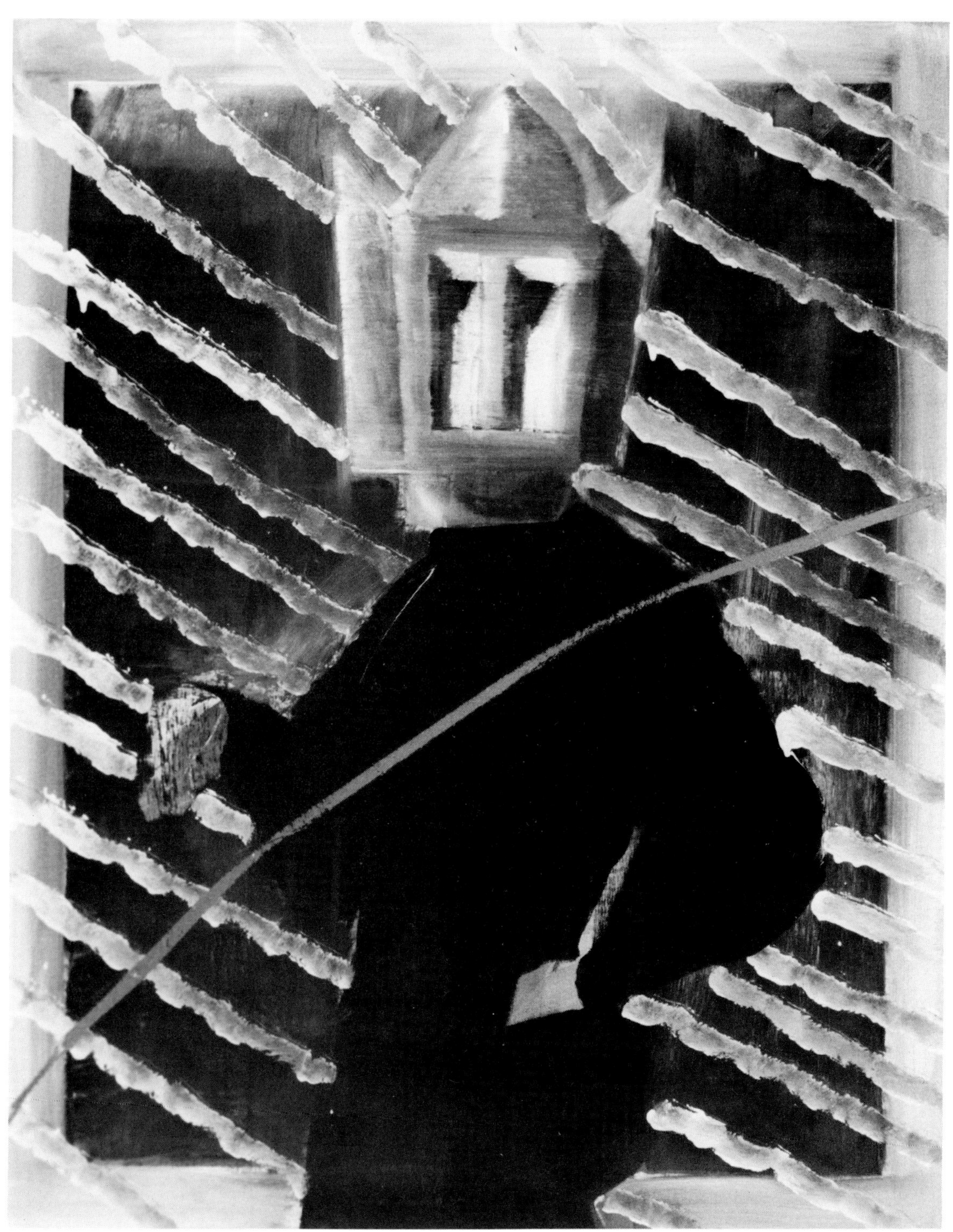

*Technician of Ecstasy #1*, 1984, oil on canvas, 44 x 34". Collection Judith Alexander.

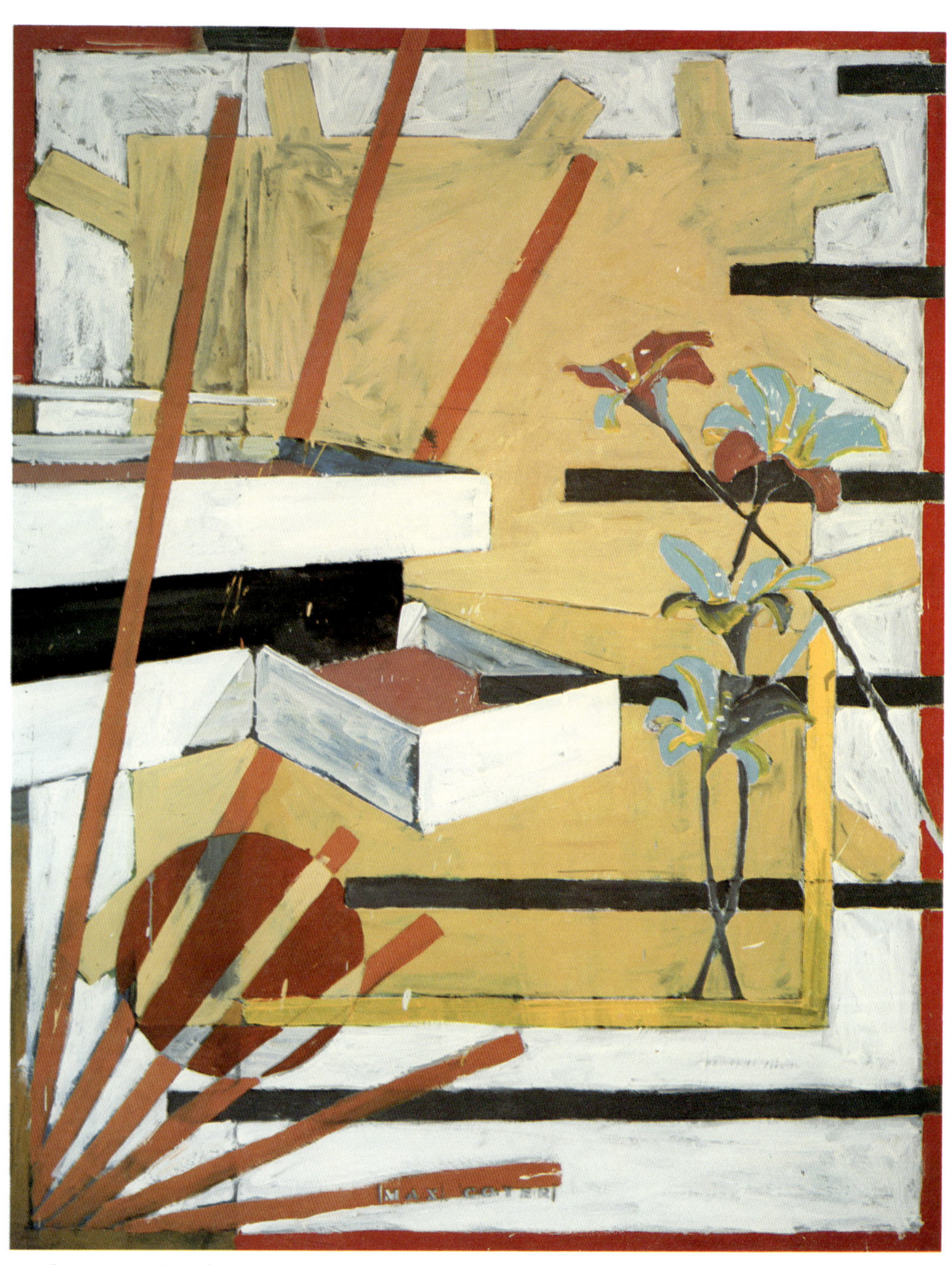

*Passage,* 1987, oil on canvas, 60 x 46 ".
Courtesy Gruenebaum Gallery, New York City.

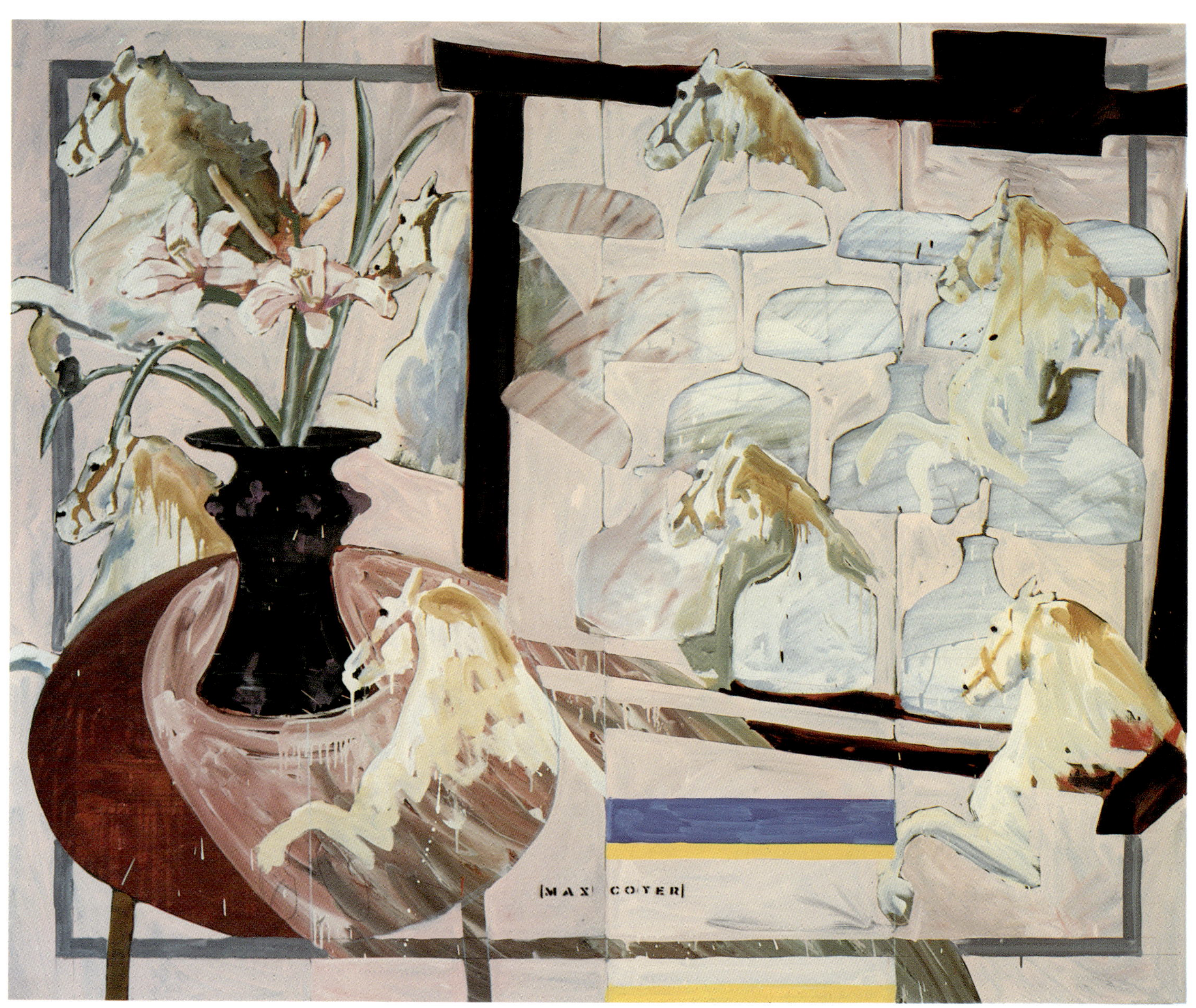



*Cloud Chamber*, 1987, oil on canvas, 60 x 72". Courtesy Gruenebaum Gallery, New York City.

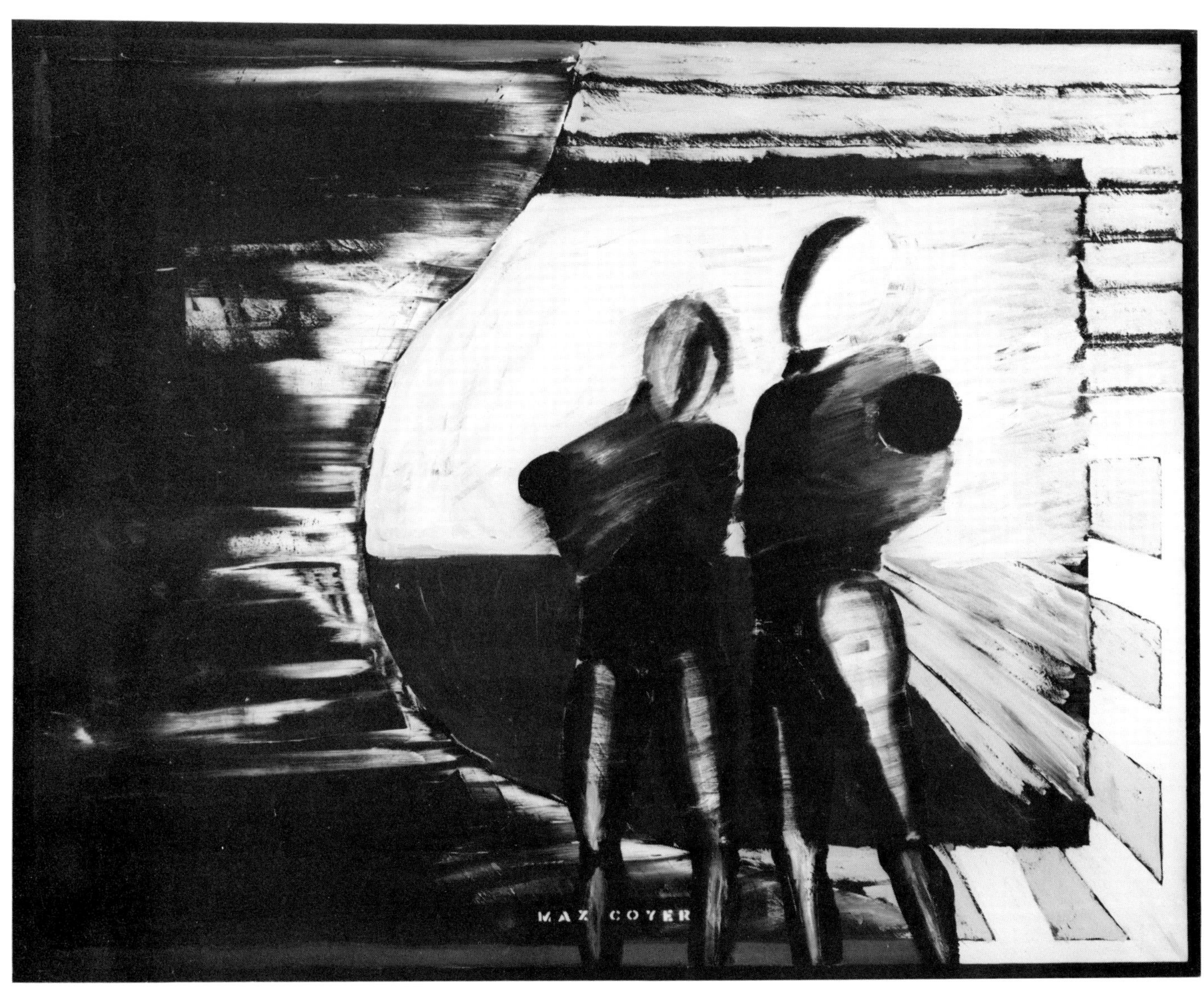


*Brutal Landscape,* 1984, oil on canvas, 48 x 60".

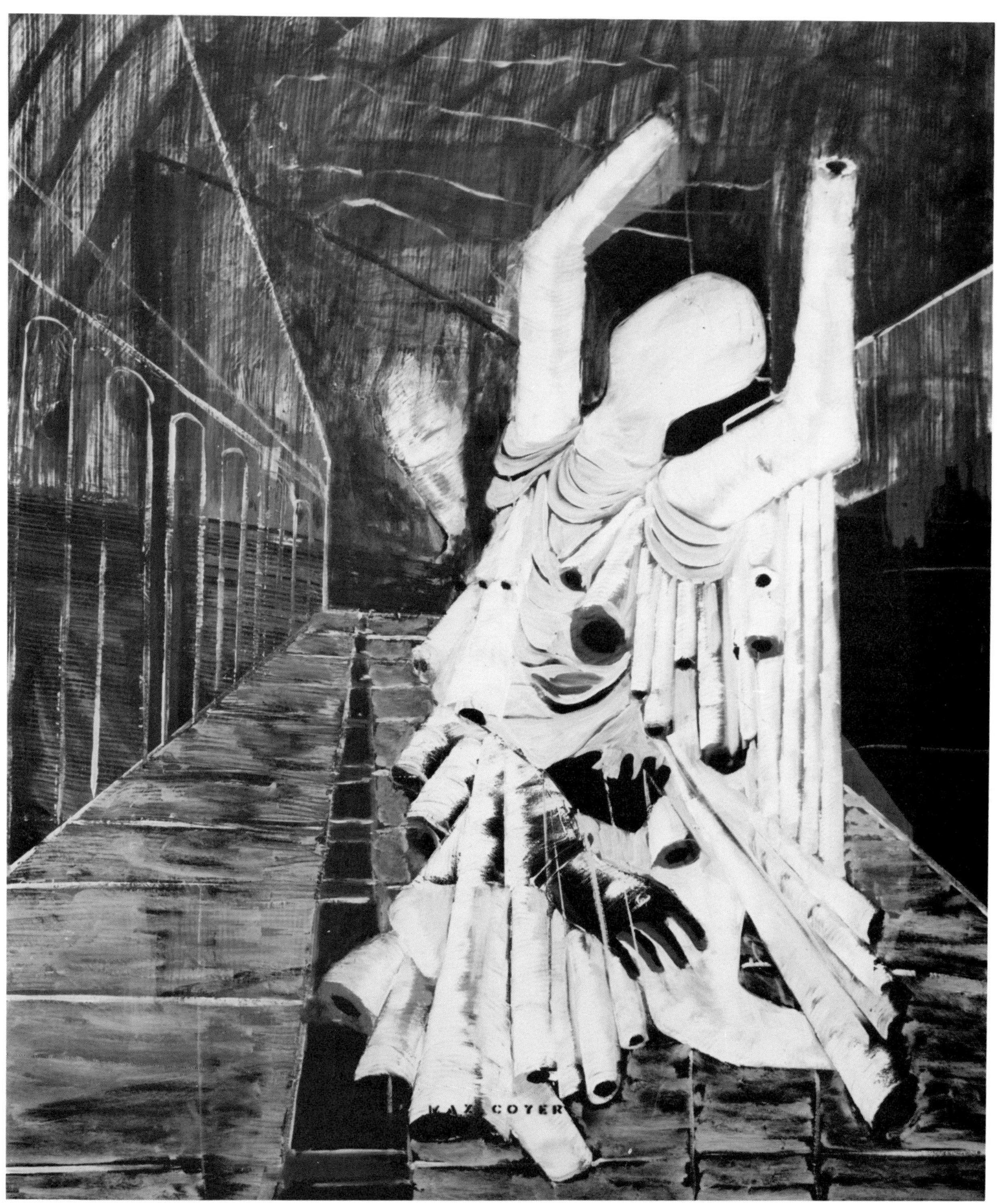

*The Death of Vitellius,* 1985, oil on canvas, 72 x 60". Collection Mr. & Mrs. William Fowler.

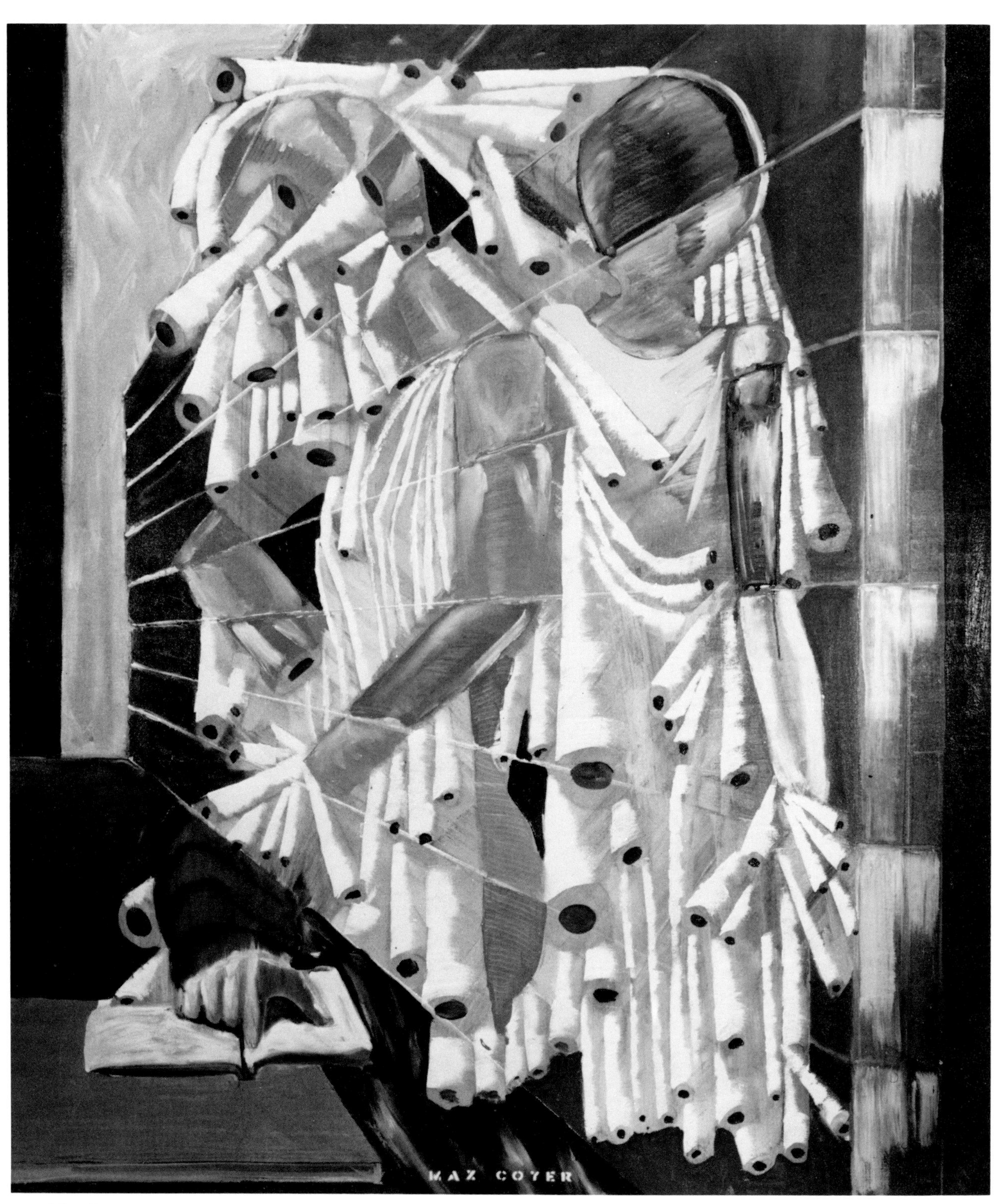

*The Barrier Offers No Resistence,* 1985, oil on canvas, 72 x 60".

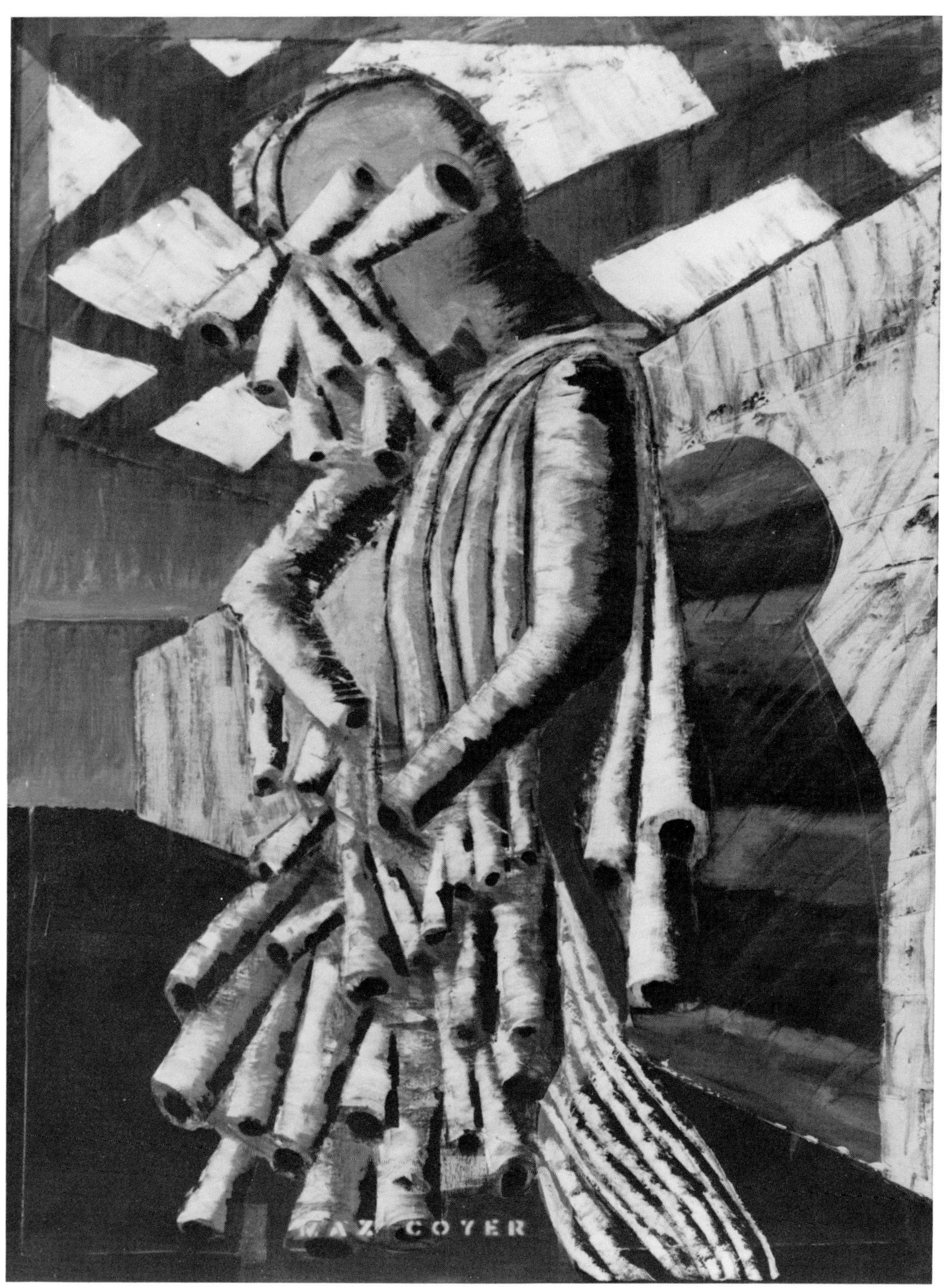


*Opium: The Fence,* 1985, oil on canvas, 46 x 34".

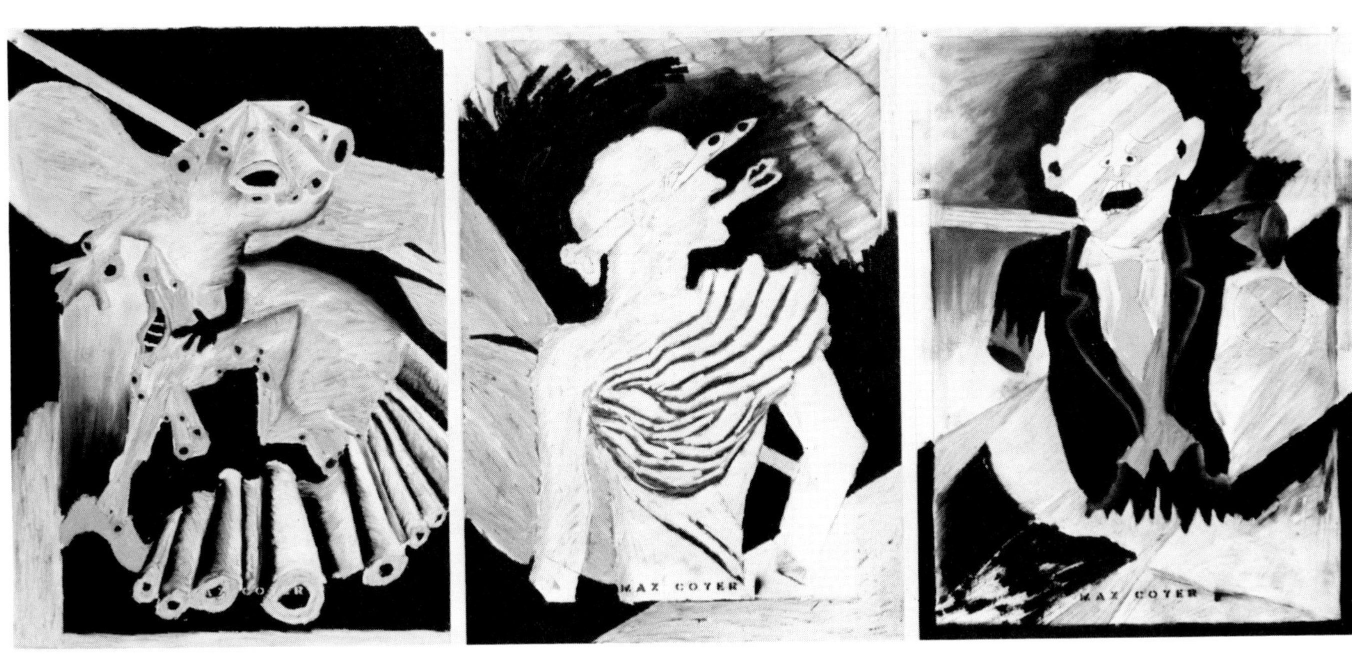

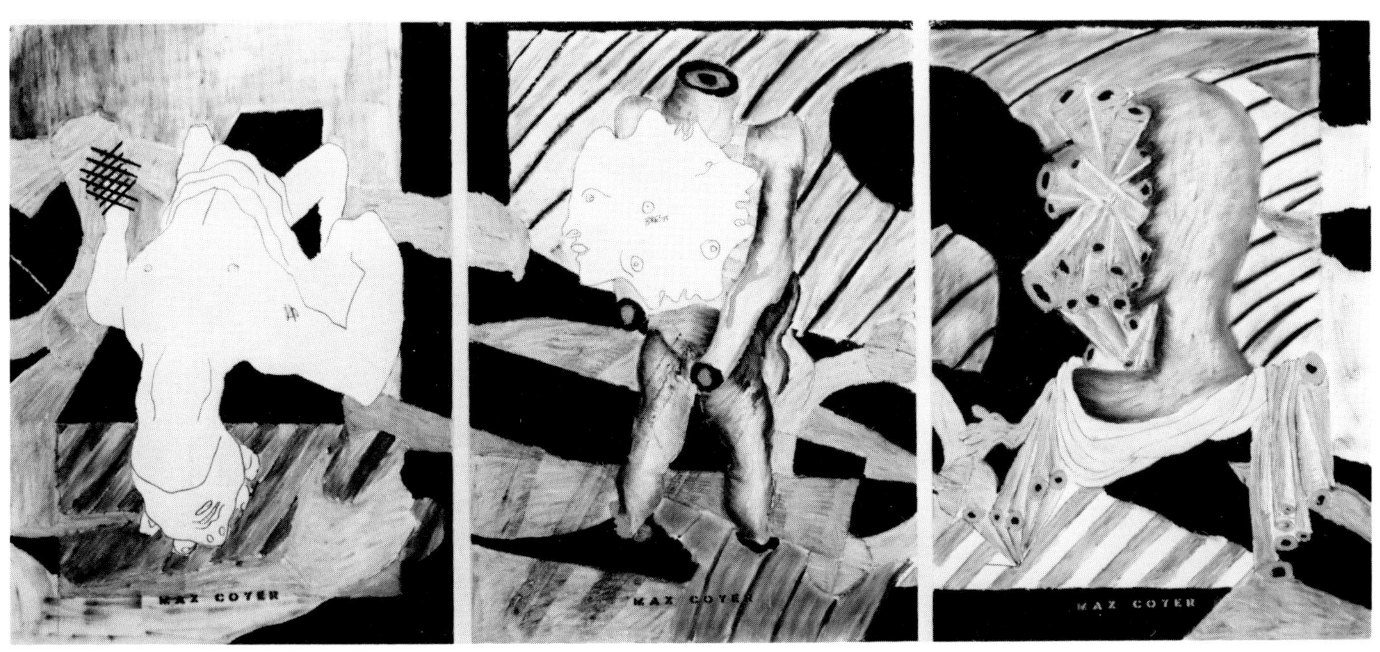



*The Opium Cycle, The First Voice* (6 panels), 1985, oilstick and pastel on paper, 43 x 30″ each page. Collection Mr. & Mrs. Steven Molasky.

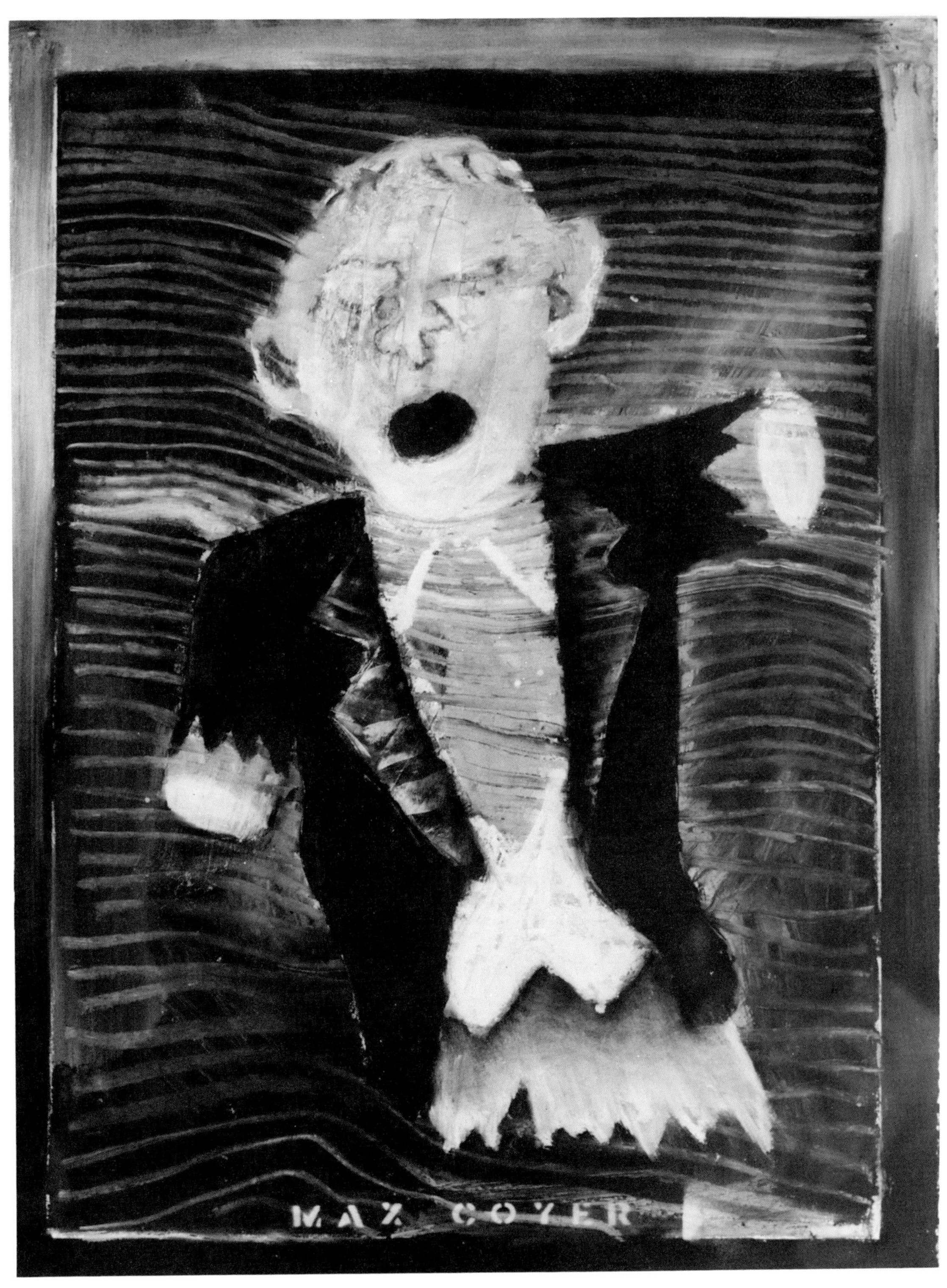


*Night Visitor,* 1985, oilstick and pastel on paper, 30 x 22". Collection The Metropolitan Museum of Art, New York City.

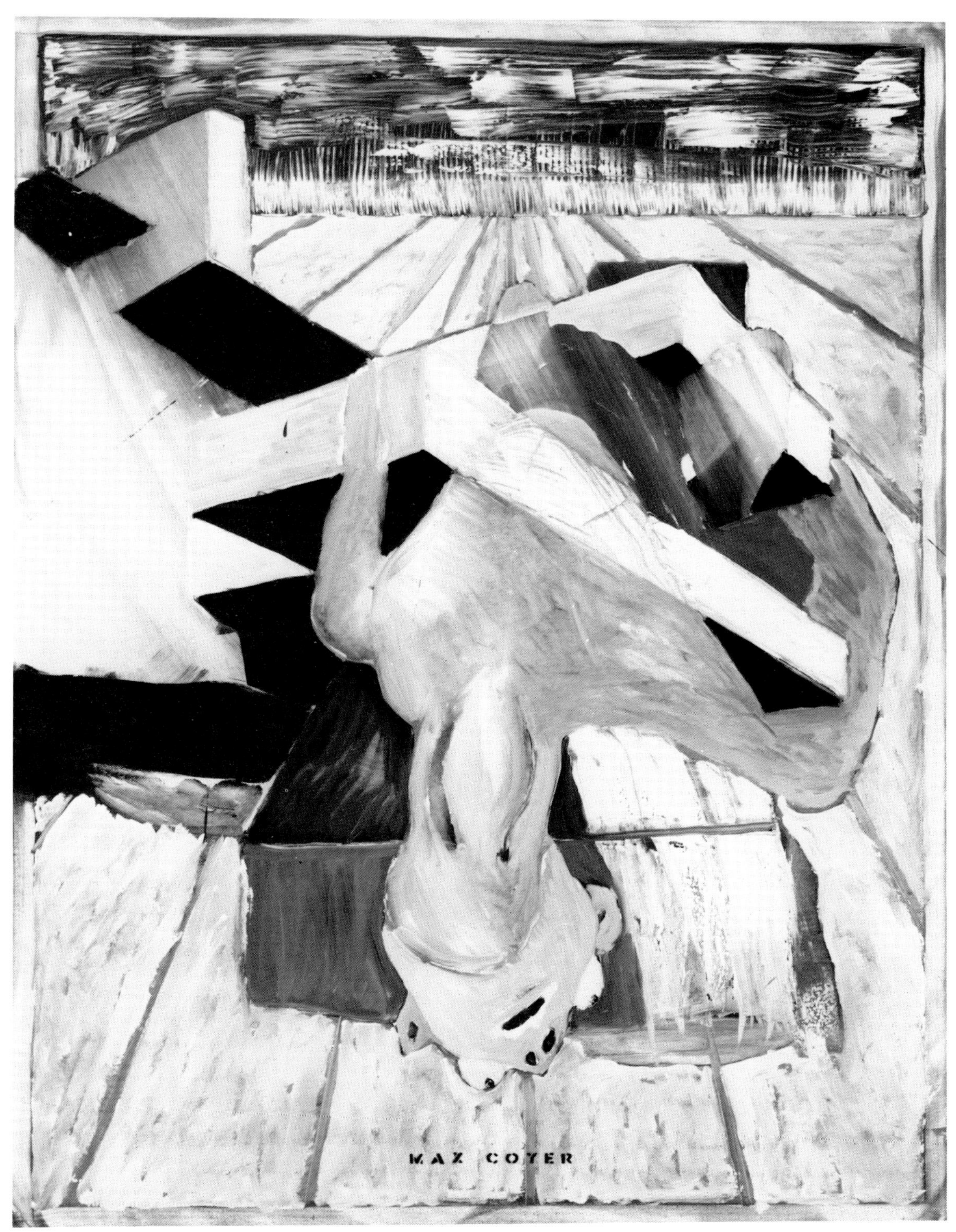



*Falling Water,* 1985, oil on canvas, 60 x 46". Private Collection.

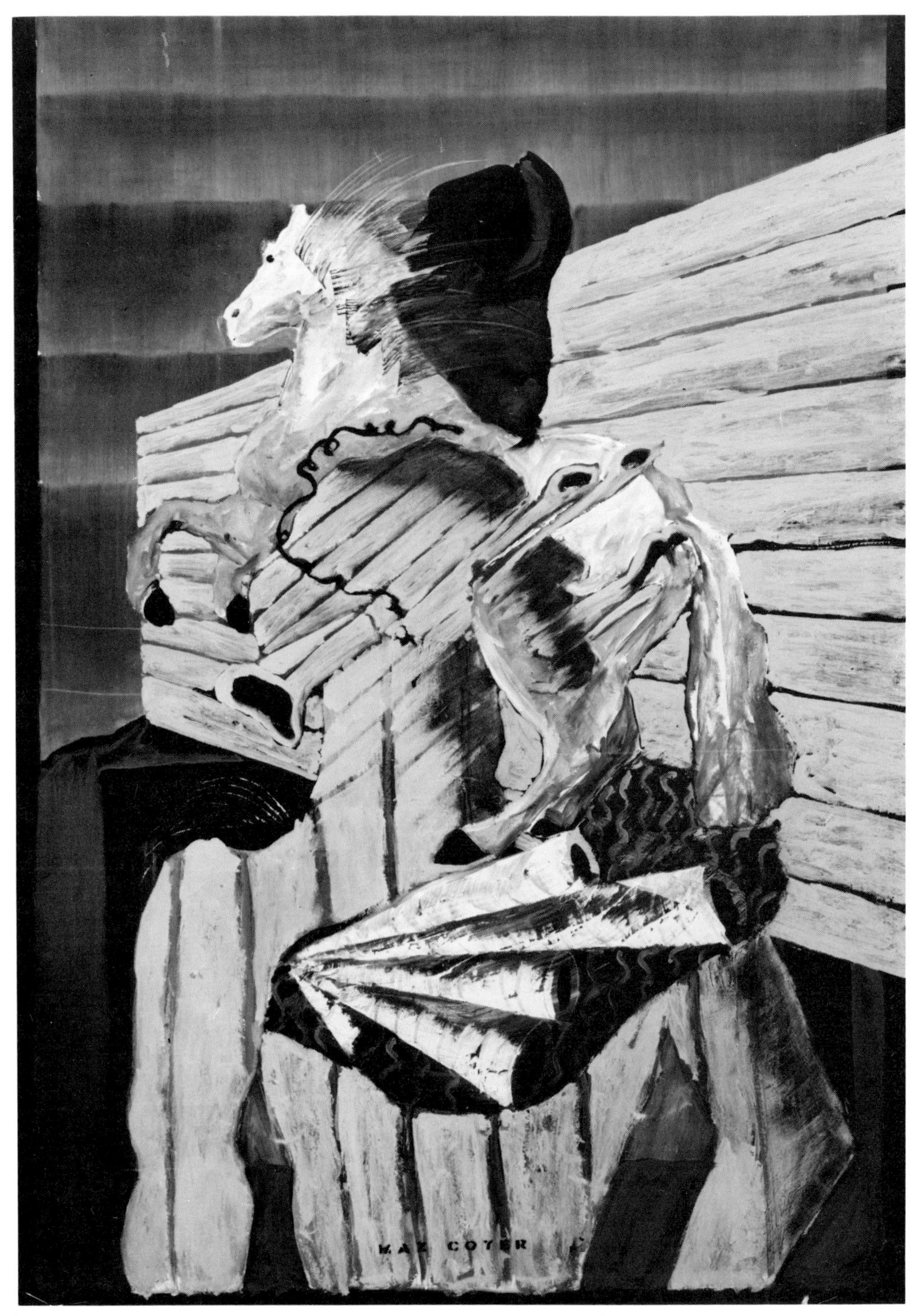

*Post Time,* oil on canvas, 70 x 48". Collection The Newark Museum, New Jersey.

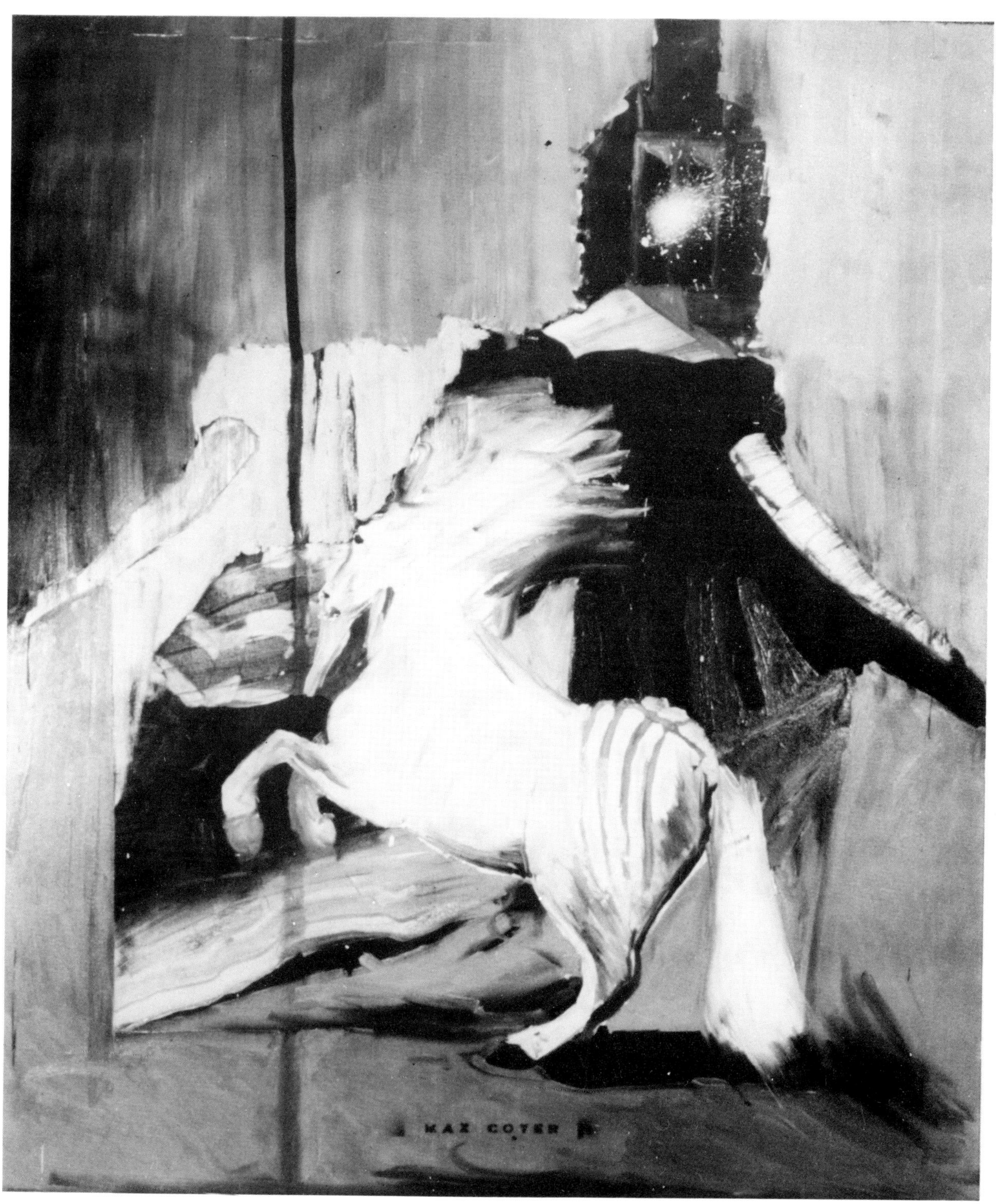

*Birthday,* 1985, oil on canvas, 72 x 60". Private Collection.

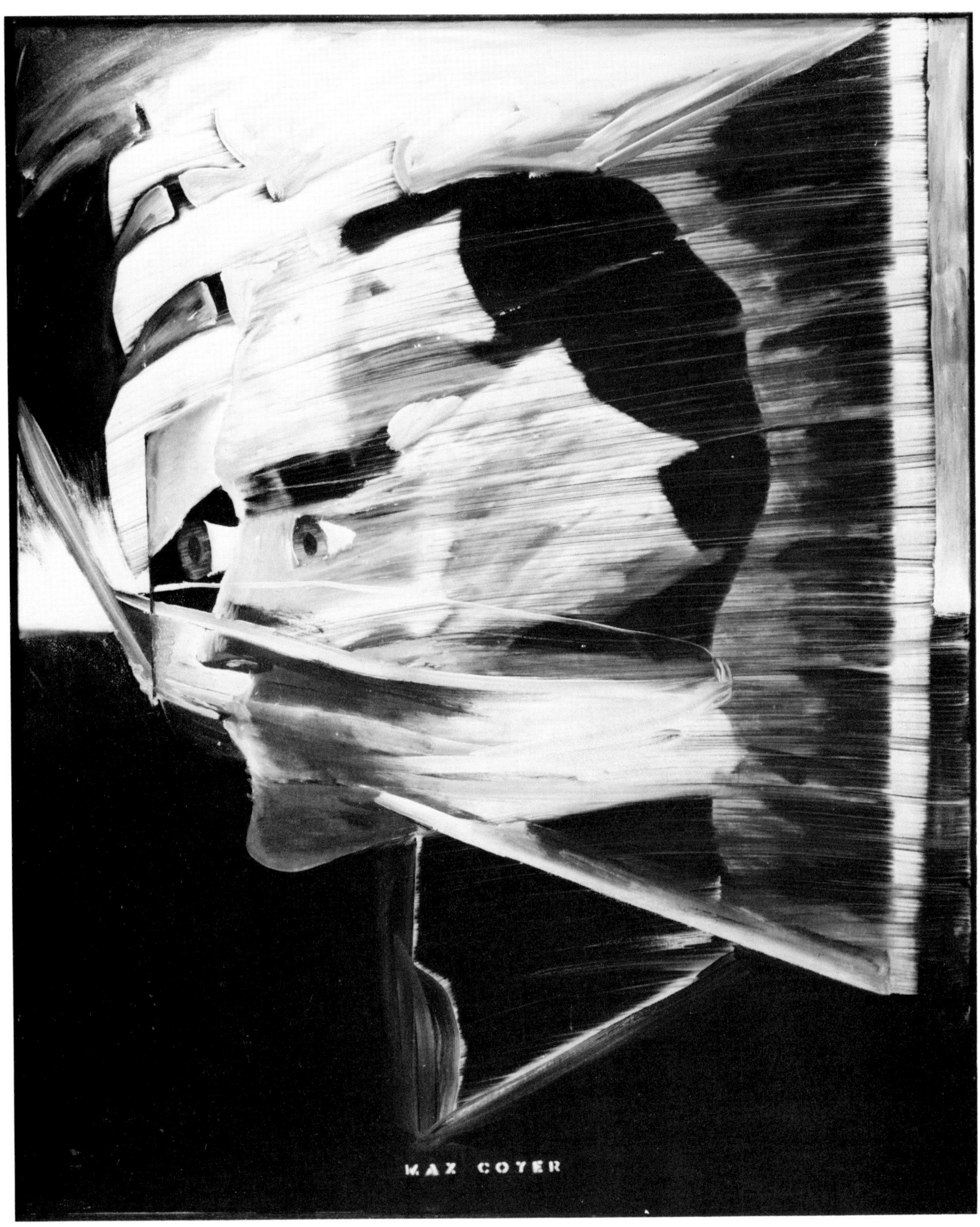



*The Dream of Nancy Sun,* 1985, oil on canvas, 60 x 48". Private Collection.

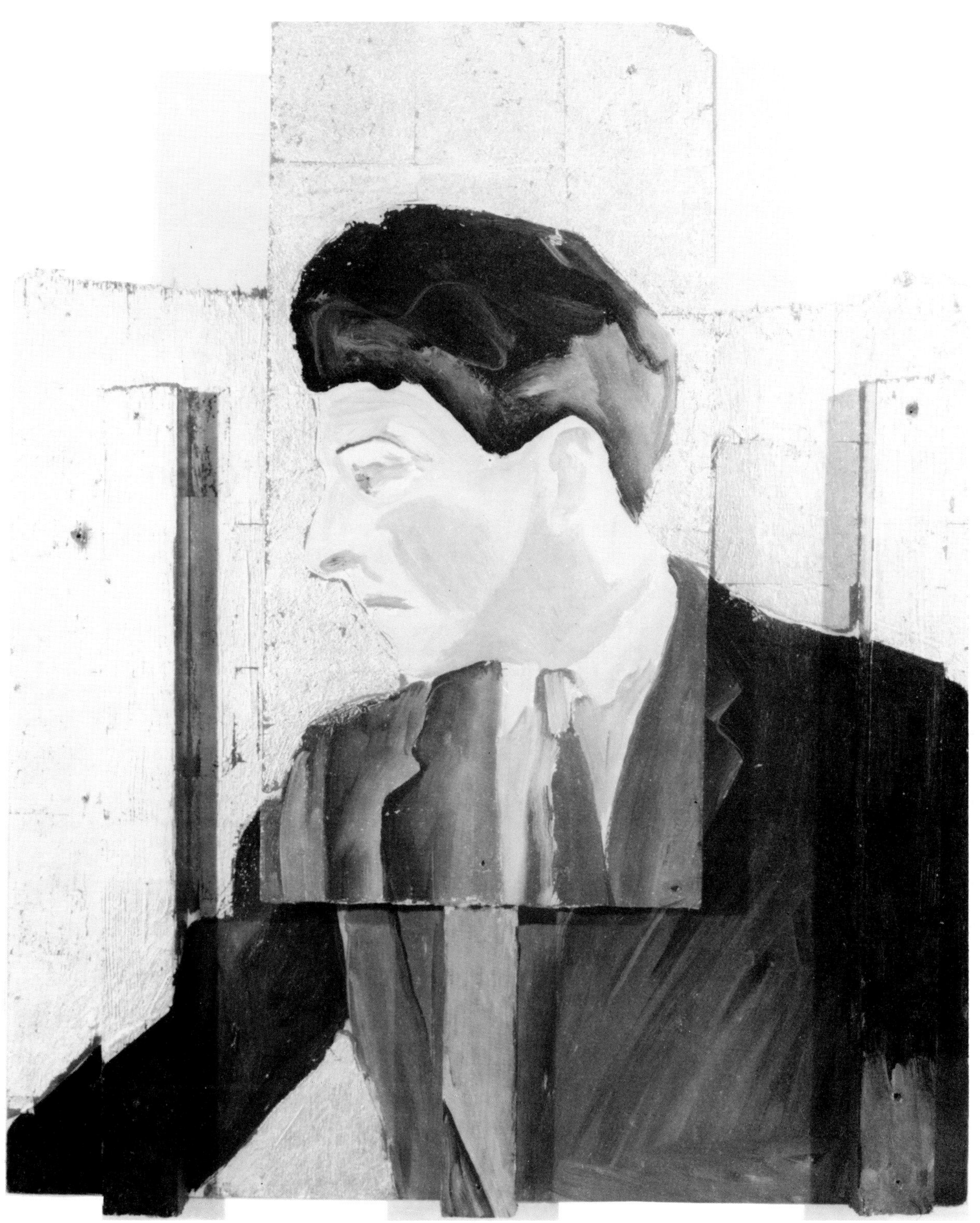

*Young Cocteau Icon,* 1985, oil on wood with gold leaf, 28 x 23″.

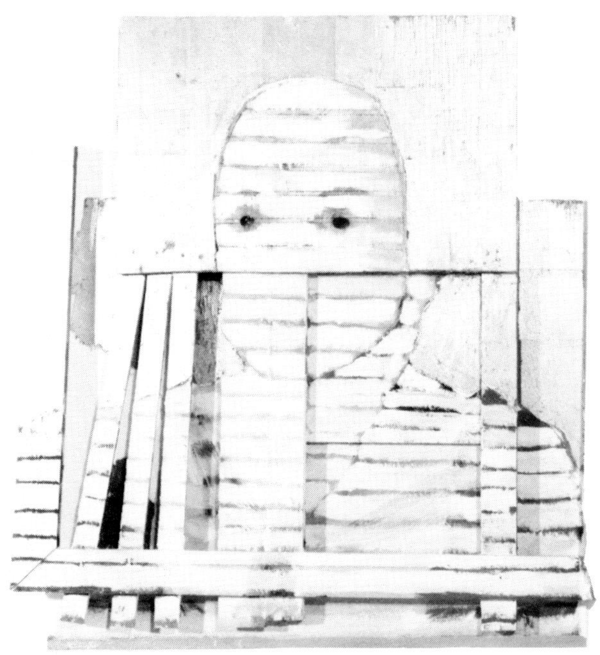

*The Chinese Princess*, 1985, oil on wood with gold leaf, 30 x 30".

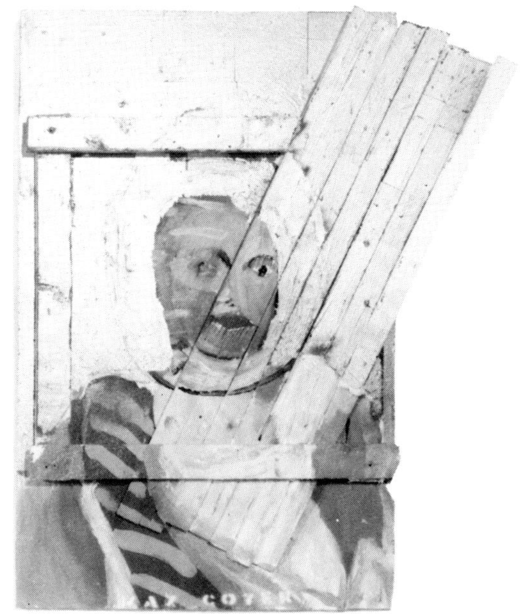

*Dauphin Icon*, 1985, oil on wood with gold leaf, 28 x 22".

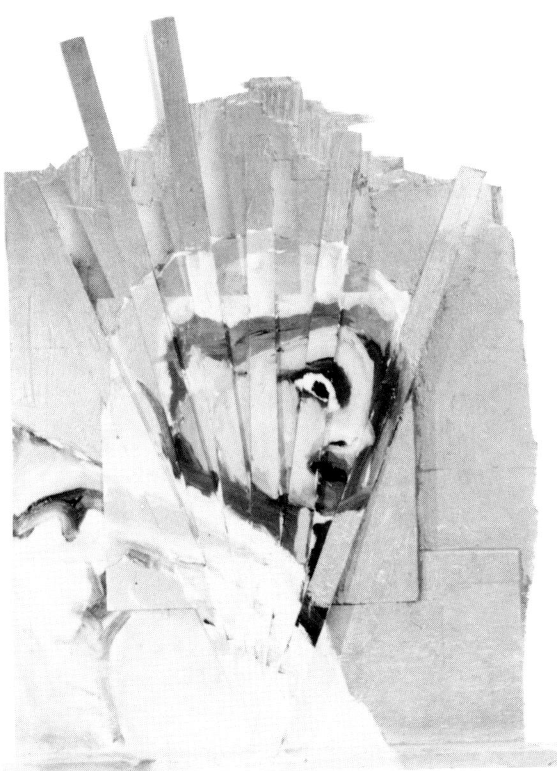

*Ingres Icon*, 1985, oil on wood with gold leaf, 32 x 23".

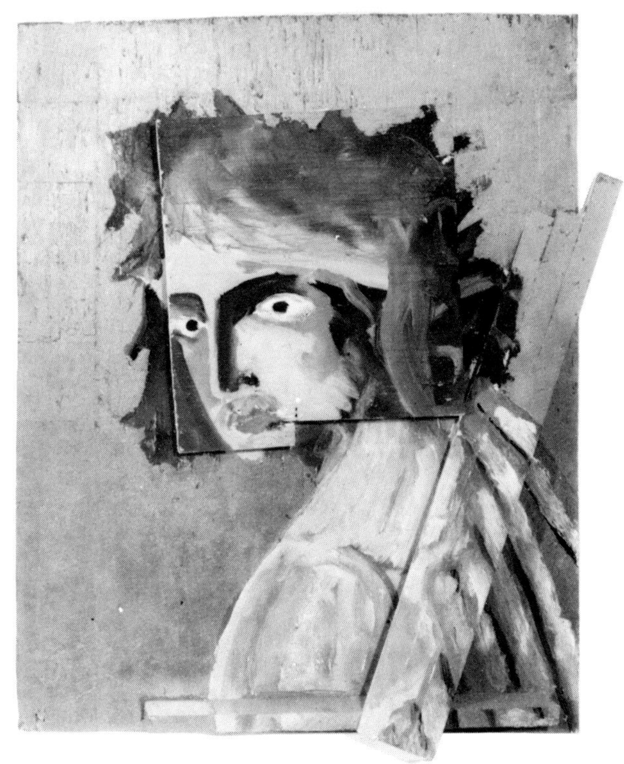

*The Sybil*, 1985, oil on wood with gold leaf, 31 x 26".

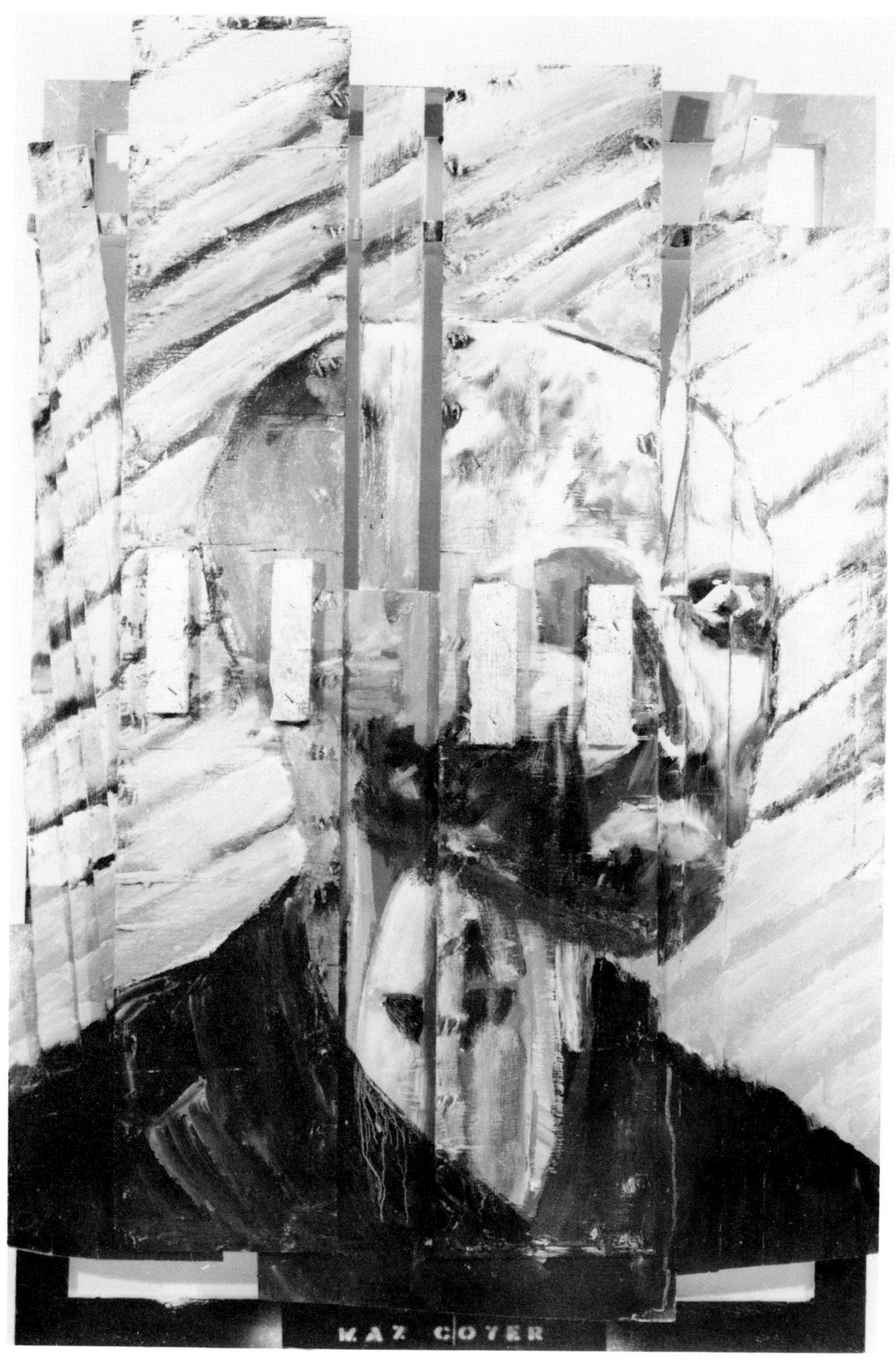



*Self-Portrait # 3*, 1985, oil on wood with gold leaf, 52 x 34 x 5".

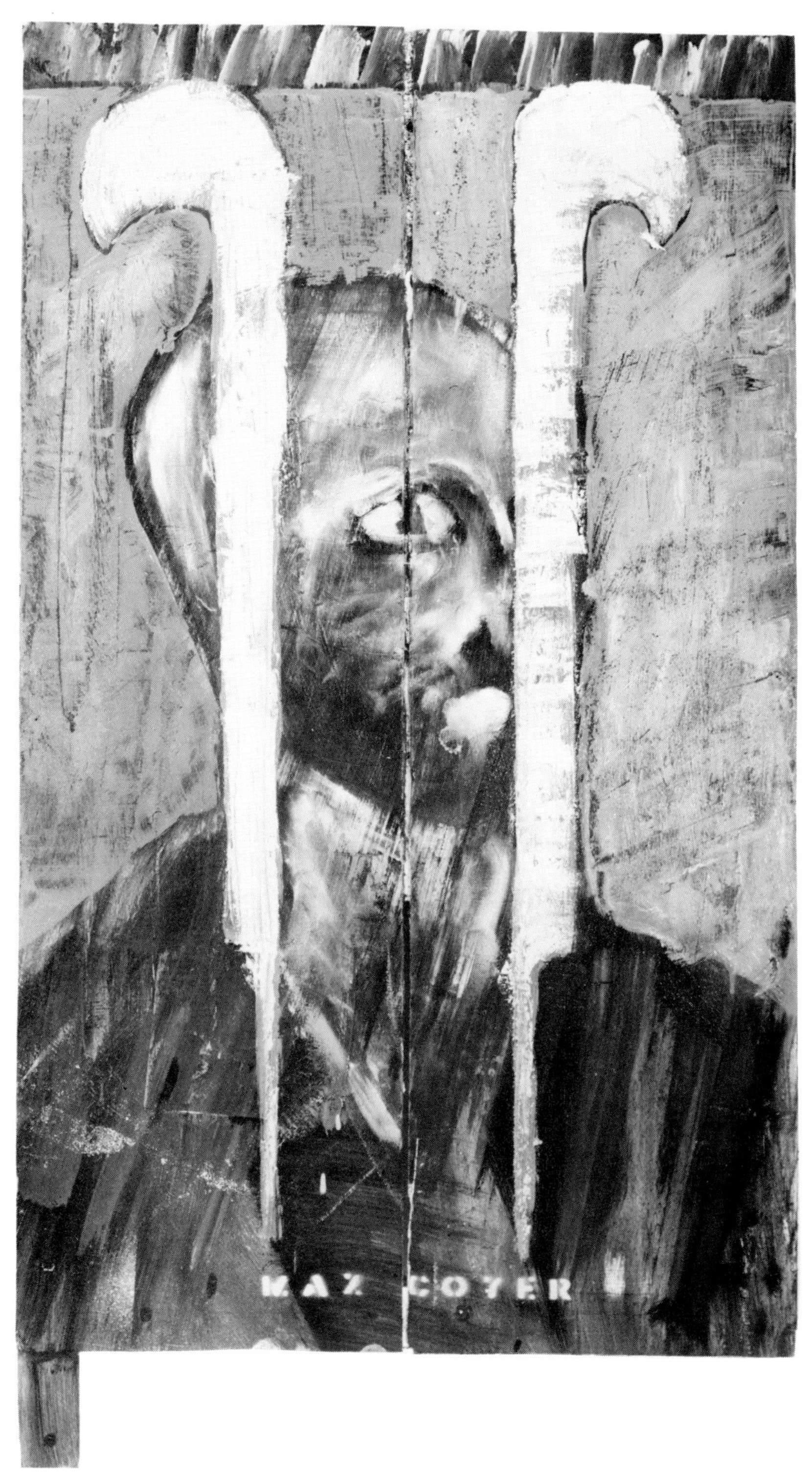

*Self-Portrait #8*, 1986, oil on wood, 37 x 20".

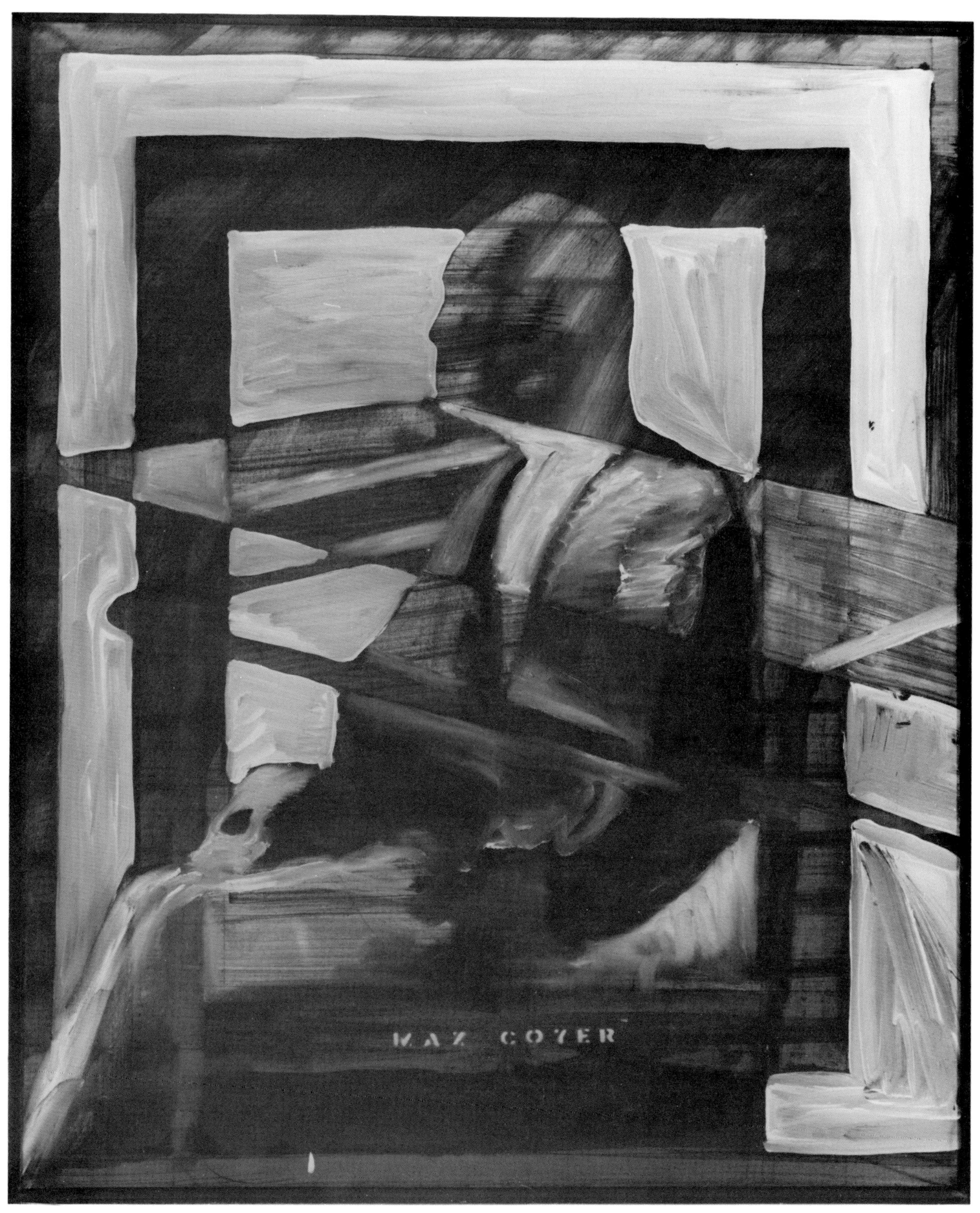



*The Glass Table* (Study for St. Peter's), 1986, oil on canvas, 42 x 34". Private Collection.

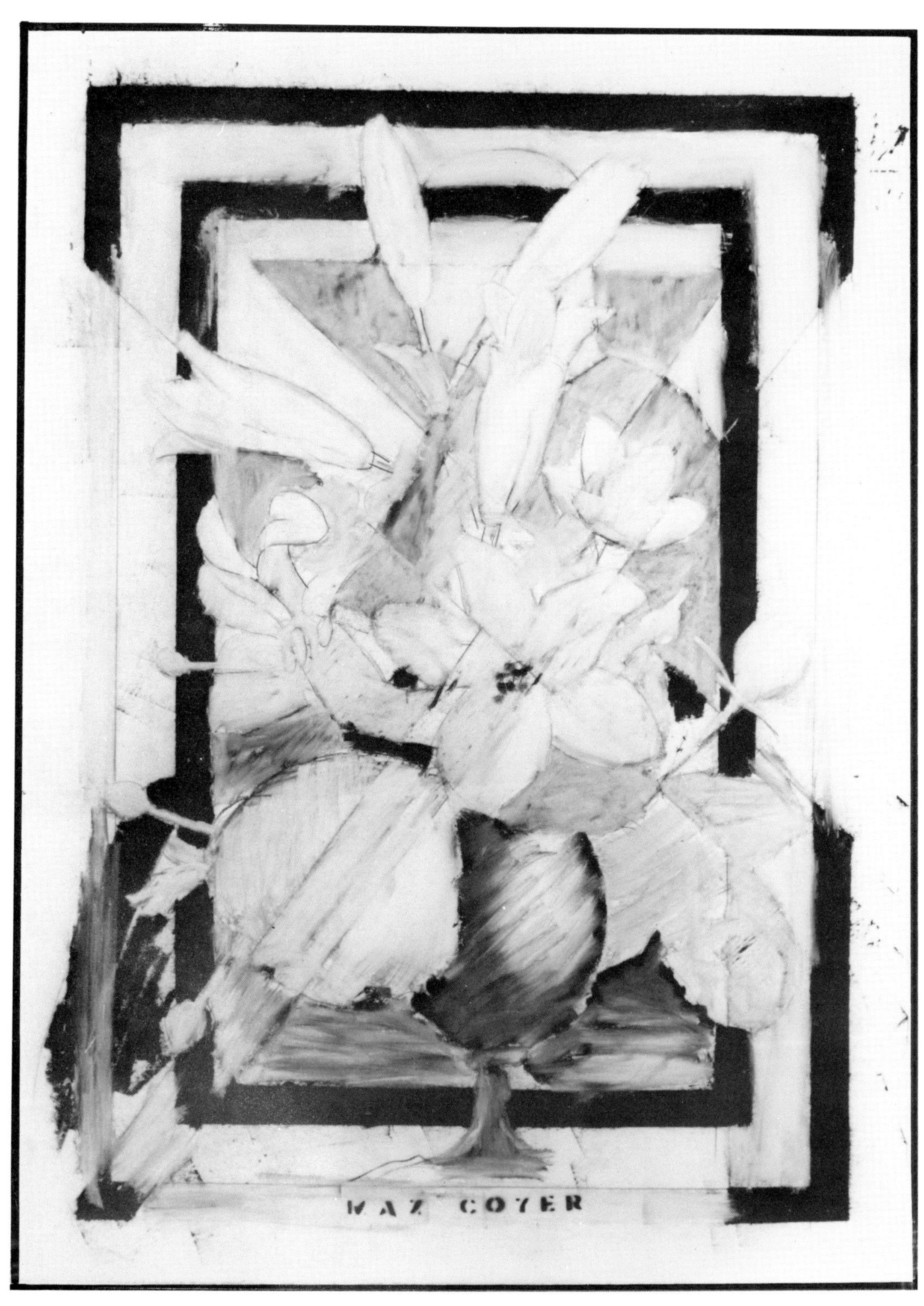


*Large Floral Study* — for St. Peter's, 1986, oilstick and pastel on paper, 40 x 30˝.
Collection Dr. & Mrs. David Rabinowitz.

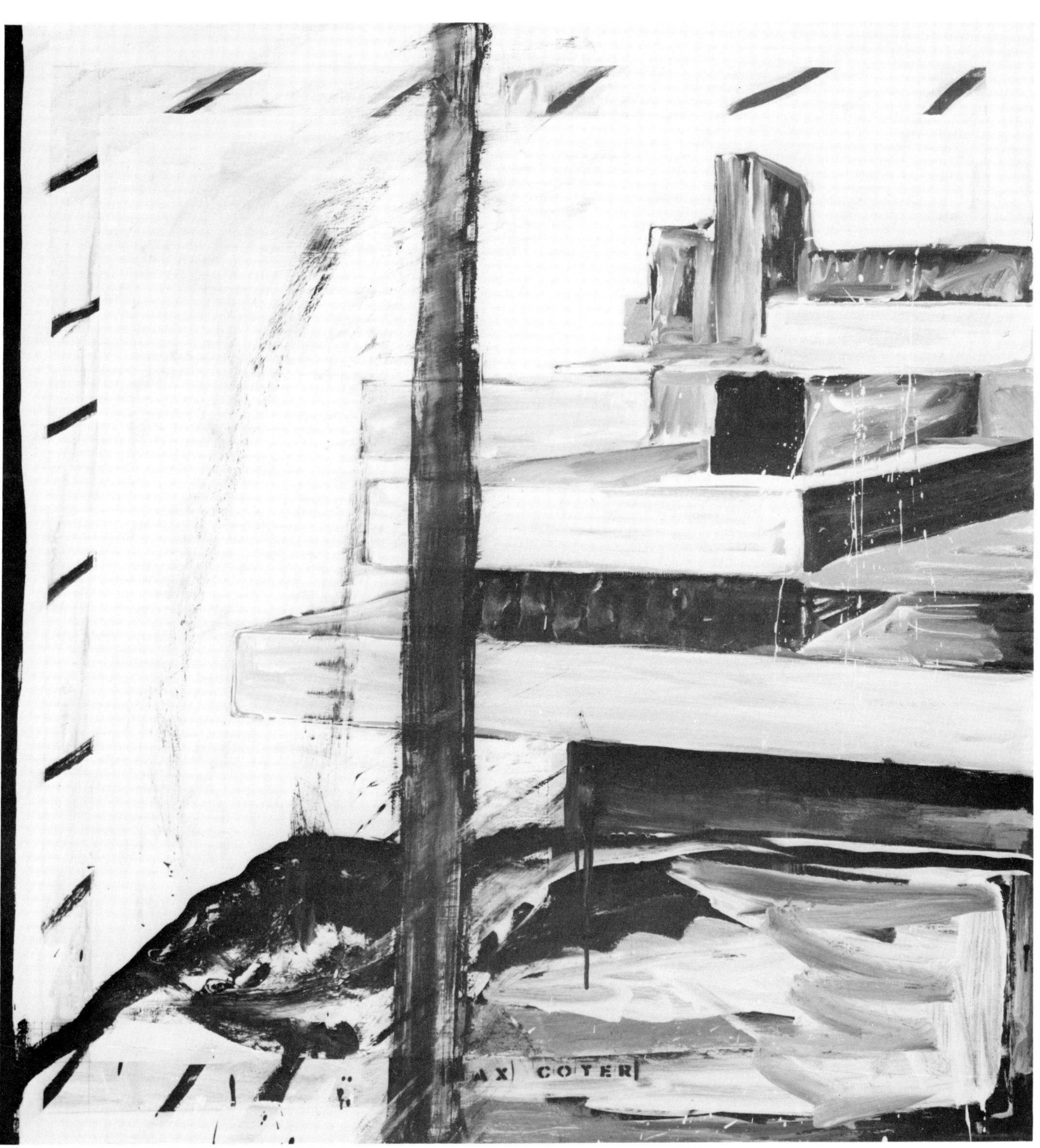


*The Tree*, 1987, oil on canvas, 50 x 46". Courtesy of Gruenebaum Gallery, New York City.

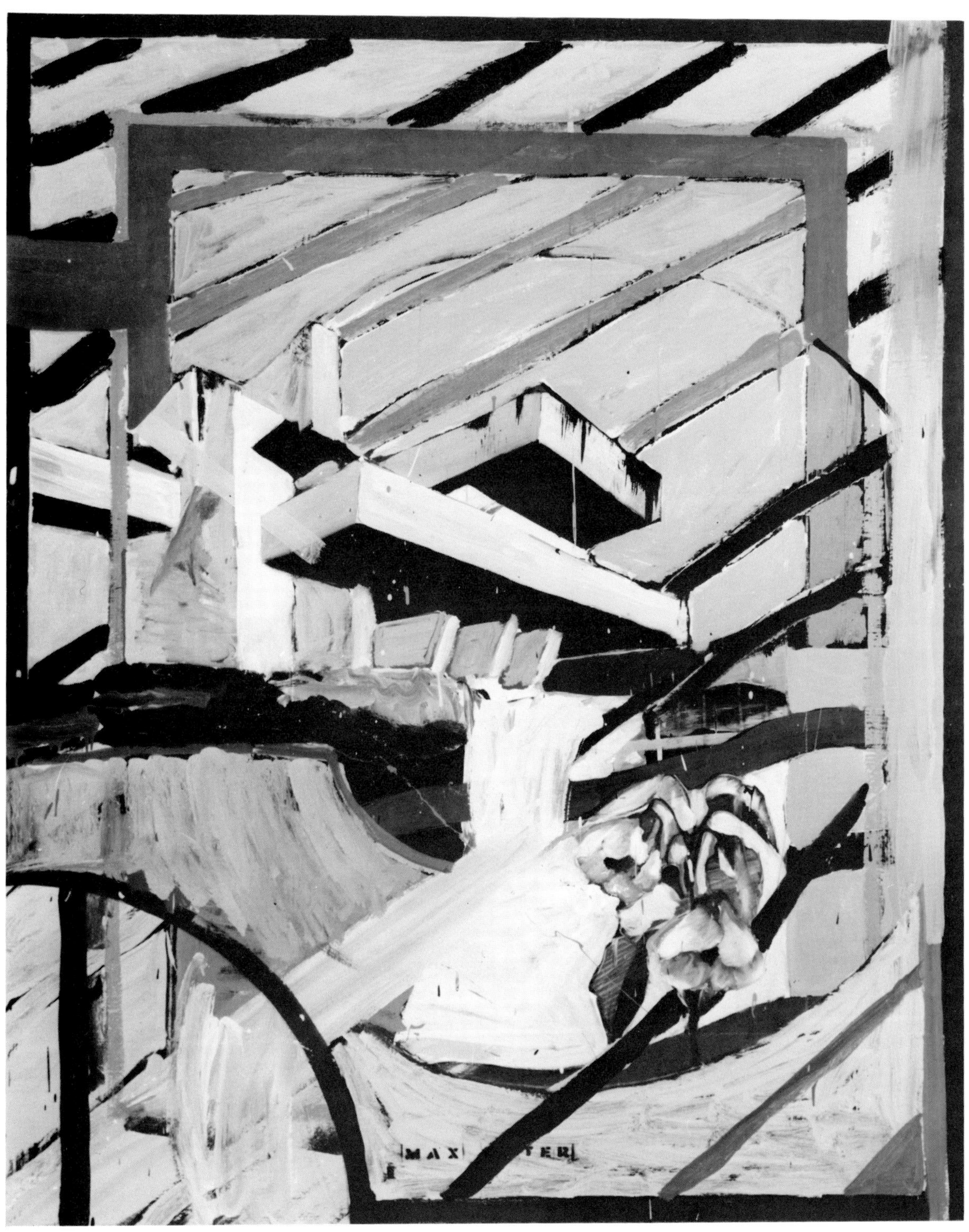

*Vulcania*, 1987, oil on canvas, 60 x 48". Courtesy Gruenebaum Gallery, New York City.

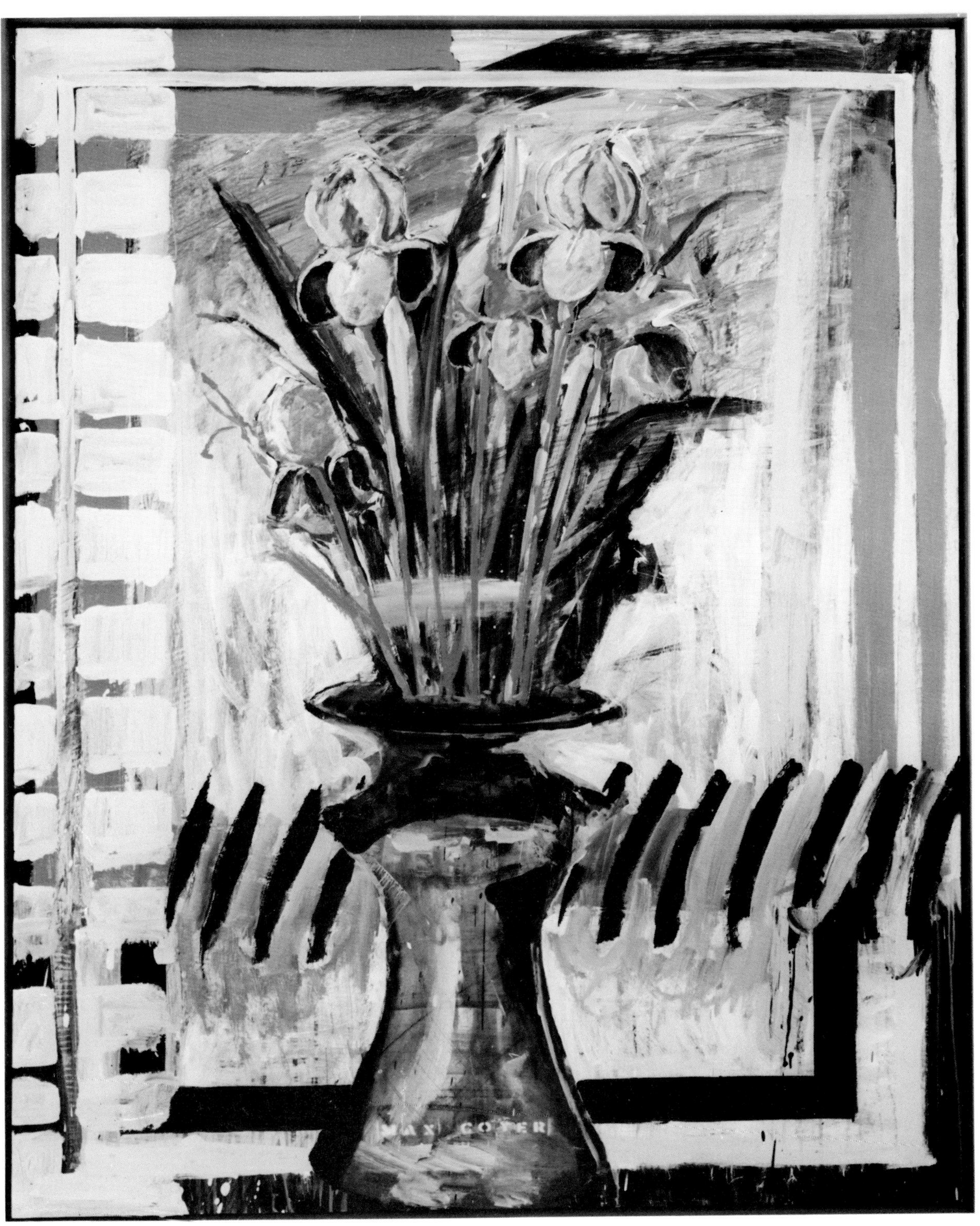

*Irises,* 1987, oil on canvas, 60 x 48". Courtesy Gruenebaum Gallery, New York City.

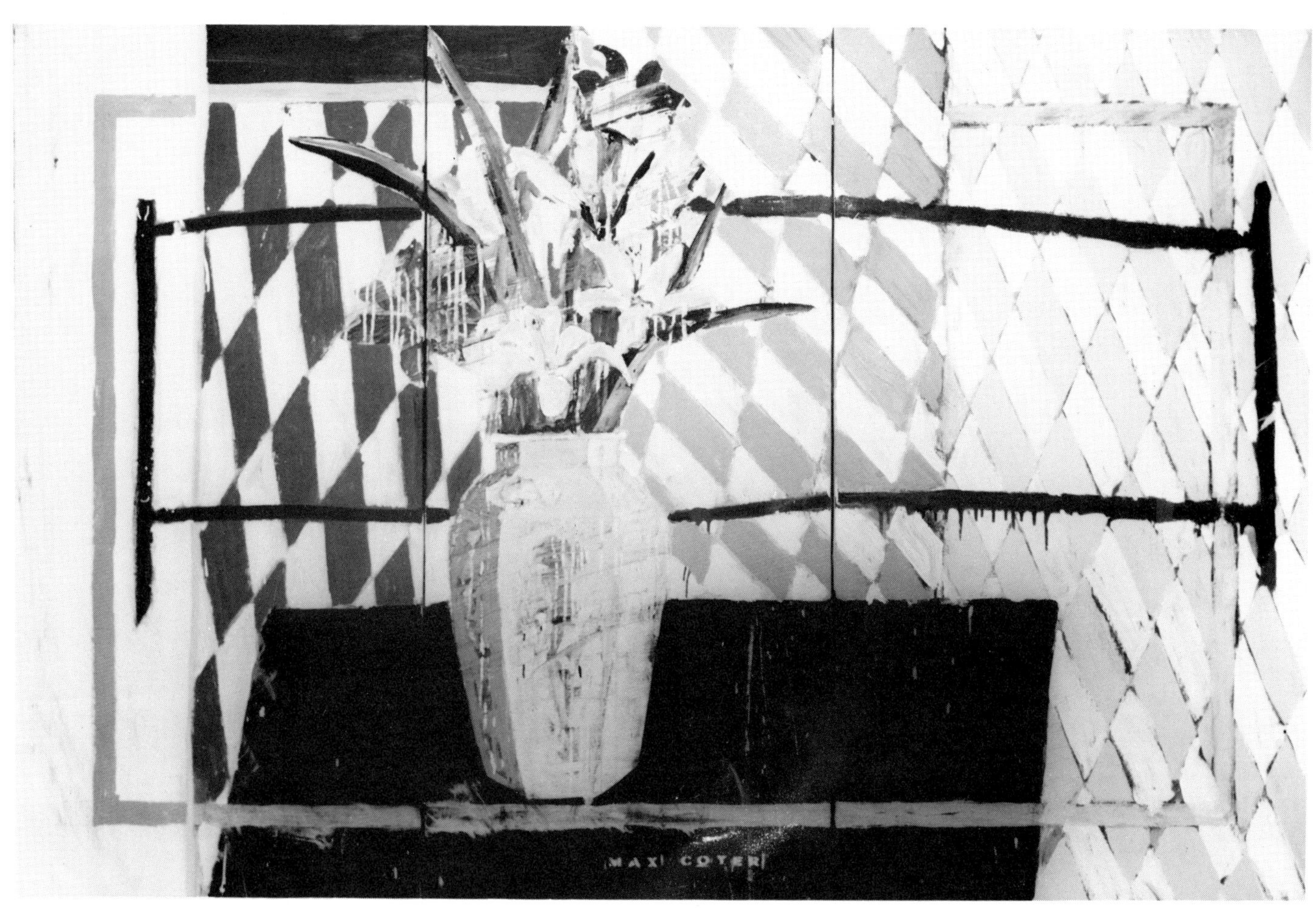


*Bridge,* 1987, oil on canvas, 48 x 70". Courtesy Gruenebaum Gallery, New York City.

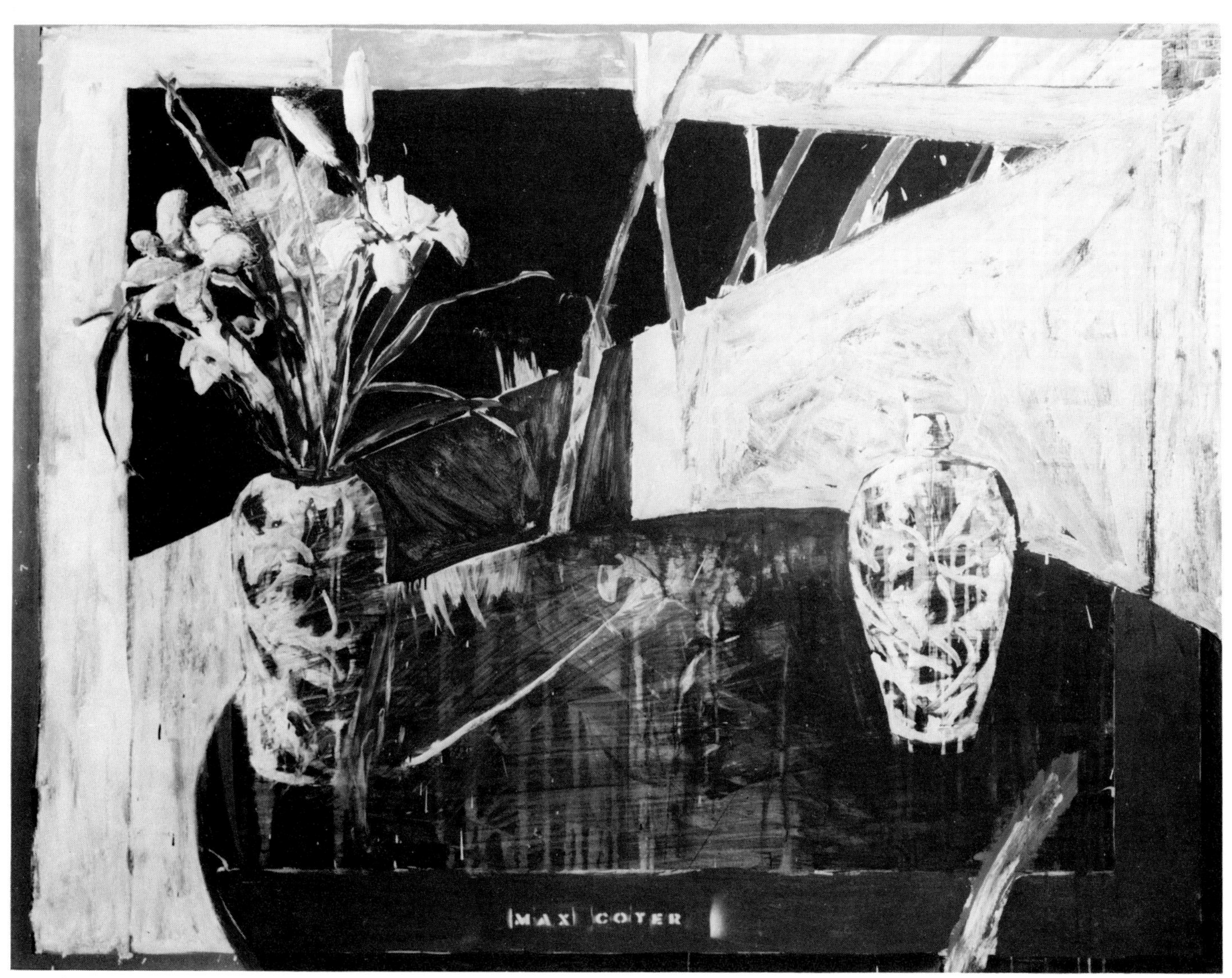



*The Proud Science,* 1987, oil on canvas, 48 x 60". Courtesy Gruenebaum Gallery, New York City.

# BIOGRAPHY

**Selected One Person Exhibitions:**
1988   Hillwood Art Gallery, Long Island University, Brookville, New York
       Fay Gold Gallery, Atlanta, Georgia
       G.H. Dalsheimer Gallery Ltd., Baltimore, Maryland
1987   Gruenebaum Gallery, New York City
1986   St. Peter's Church, New York City
       Michael Kohn Gallery, Los Angeles, California
       Fay Gold Gallery, Atlanta, Georgia
       M-13 Gallery, New York City
1985   Harm Bouckaert Gallery, New York City
       Klein Gallery, Chicago, Illinois
1984   Harm Bouckaert Gallery, New York City (October)
       Harm Bouckaert Gallery, New York City (January)
1983   Harm Bouckaert Gallery, New York City (Photography)
1982   Harm Bouckaert Gallery, New York City

**Selected Group Exhibitions:**
1987   "Realism and Abstraction: Twentieth Century American Art in the Newark
       Museum," Newark Museum, New Jersey.
       Gallery Group Show, Gruenebaum Gallery, New York City
1986   "Recently Acquired Contemporary Paintings," Newark Museum, New Jersey
       Group Show, Members' Gallery, Albright-Knox Museum, Buffalo, New York.
       "A Second Talent: Painters & Sculptors Who Are Also Photographers," Baruch
       College Gallery, New York City, (organized by the Aldrich Museum)
       "8 x 10," Washington County Museum of Fine Arts, Maryland
       "The Liberty Show," Neo Persona, New York City
       "Heads," Mokotoff Gallery, New York City
       "Painting in the 3rd Dimension," City Without Walls, Newark, New Jersey
1985   "A Second Talent: Painters & Sculptors Who Are Also Photographers," The Aldrich
       Museum of Contemporary Art, Ridgefield, Connecticut
       "Basically Boxes," Klein Gallery, Chicago, Illinois
       Group Show, Members' Gallery, Albright-Knox Museum, Buffalo, New York.
       "Reliefs and Mobiles," Tower Gallery, New York City
       "The Doll Show: Artists' Dolls and Figurines," Hillwood Art Gallery, Long Island
       University, Brookville, New York
       Neo Persona Gallery, New York City
       Lillian Heidenberg Gallery, New York City
       Chicago International Art Expo, Klein Gallery, Chicago, Illinois
1984   Klein Gallery, Chicago, Illinois
       Group Show, Members' Gallery, Albright-Knox Museum, Buffalo, New York.
       "Eccentric Images," Margo Leavin Gallery, Los Angeles, California
       "Bacchanalia," New York Public Library, New York City
       "Miniatures," Lillian Heidenberg Gallery, New York City
       "Synthetic Art, The Big Show," Harm Bouckaert Gallery, New York City
       "L'Esprit Encyclopedic," New York Public Library, New York City
       "Extravaganza," Dramatis Personae, New York City
1983   "Saints," Harm Bouckaert Gallery, New York City
       "Work 4 the Next Revolution," Harm Bouckaert Gallery, New York City
       "Painting from the Mind's Eye," Hillwood Art Gallery, Long Island University,
       Brookville, New York

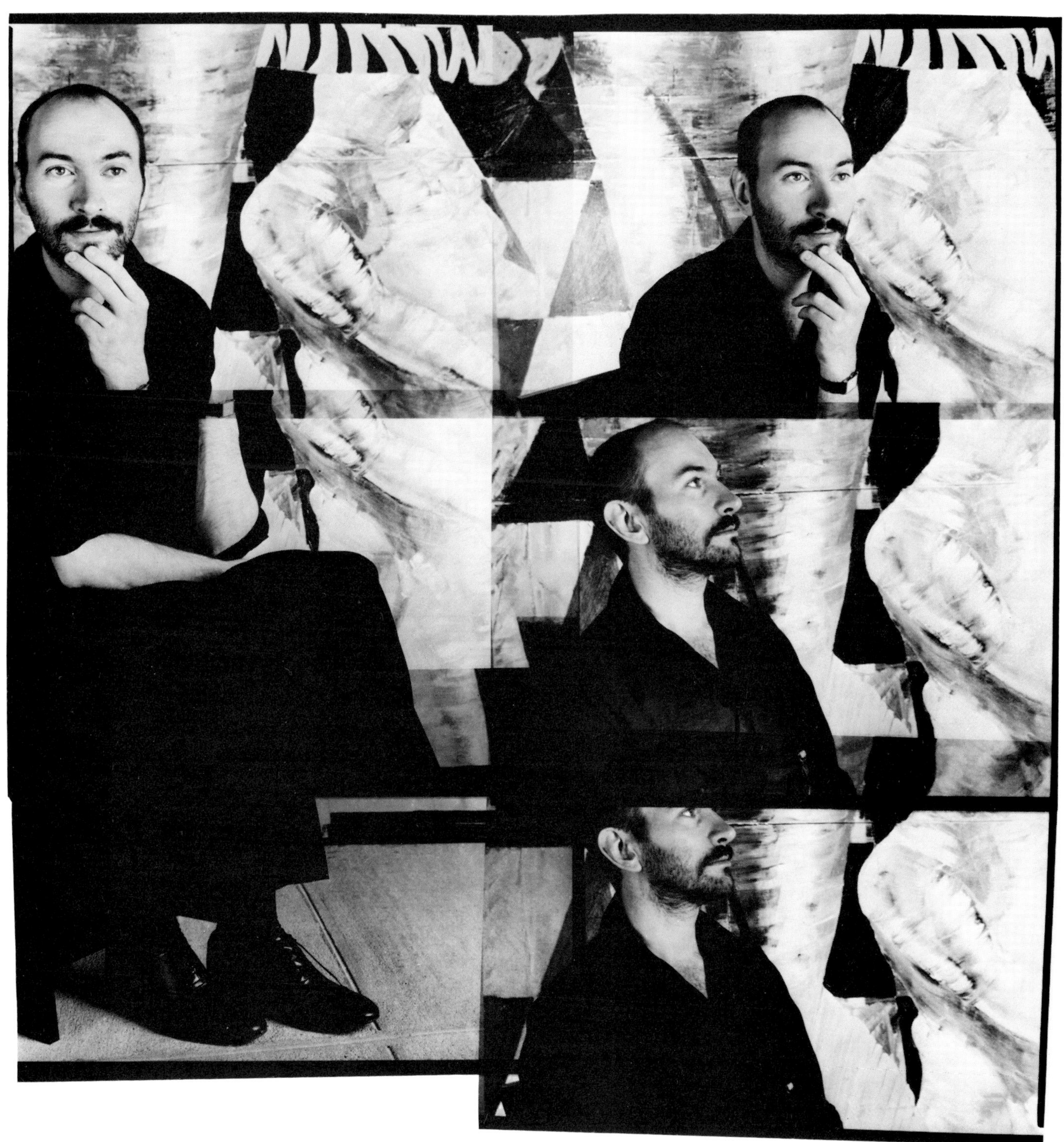

Max Coyer. Photo: Christopher Makos.

1980   "Objects," Alonzo Gallery, New York City
       "Glitter," Kathryn Markel Gallery, New York City
       "Works on Paper," Alonzo Gallery, New York City
1979   "Still Life," Lamont Gallery, Phillips Exeter Academy, New Hampshire
       "New American Still Life," Westmoreland County Museum of Art, Pennsylvania
       "Collages-Watercolors-Drawings," Alonzo Gallery, New York City

## Selected Public Collections:

The Metropolitan Museum of Art, New York City
The Chase Manhattan Bank, New York City
The Newark Museum, New Jersey
Zimmerli Art Museum, Rutgers University, New Jersey
Bank of America, San Francisco, California
Best Products, Richmond, Virginia
Hospital Corporation of America, Nashville, Tennessee
Shearson-Lehman Brothers, New York City
Siemens Capital Corporation, New York City
Price Carnahan, Atlanta
Linklaters & Paines, New York City

## Selected Bibliography:


*Art and Antiques*, "Openings," May 1986.
Artner, Alan G. Review, *Chicago Tribune*, March 15, 1986.
Cotter, Holland. *Arts*, April 1983.
    . *Arts*, June 1984.
Di Felice, Attanasio. Catalogue essay, "New Paintings: (the recovery of jean cocteau)," October 1985.
Henry, Gerrit. Review, *Art News*, February 1986.
King, Dora. "Atlanta," *New Art International*, Summer 1986.
Makos, Christopher. "In New York City, Around Town," *Interview*, June 1984.
Martin, Richard. "Max Coyer," *Arts*, October 1985.
Metzger, Robert. Introduction to catalogue: "New Paintings: (the recovery of jean cocteau)," October 1985.
    . "Profile — Max Coyer," *Gallery Guide*, October 1985.
Sofer, Ken. Review, *Art News*, February 1985.
Tatransky, Valentin. Review, *Arts*, January 1983.
Upshaw, Reagan. Review, *Art in America*, January 1986.
Van Wagner, Judy. "Max Coyer: Sacred and Profane Art," catalogue essay, "The Endless Voyage: Death and Transfiguration," St. Peter's Church, New York City, October 1986.
    . "Max Coyer's Painted Life of the Mind," *Arts*, January 1984.
    . "Painting from the Mind's Eye," catalogue essay, Long Island University, 1983.
    . "A Radical Idea: An Interview with Max Coyer," *Arts*, September 1984.
Volmer, Suzanne. Review, *Arts*, December 1983.
Westfall, Stephan. Review, *Arts*, September 1983.


## Awards:

Krasner-Pollock Foundation award, 1987.

## Gallery Representation:

Gruenebaum Gallery Ltd., 415 West Broadway, NYC 10012 (212) 966-3646
Fay Gold Gallery, 3221 Cains Hill Place, Atlanta, GA. 30305 (404) 233-3843
G.H. Dalsheimer Gallery Ltd., 336 North Charles Street, Baltimore, Maryland 21201 (301) 727-0866